IN GOD'S CROSSHAIRS

• A DAILY DEVOTIONAL FOR HUNTERS •

By Bob Green

TATE PUBLISHING, LLC

Published in the United States of America
by Tate Publishing, LLC
127 East Trade Center Terrace
Mustang, OK 73064
(888) 361–9473

All Scripture quotations taken from the *Holy Bible, King James Version,* Cambridge, 1769.

ISBN: 1–5988640–0-9

FOREWORD

It is hard to imagine that getting one short email message could make such an impact on a person. In, mid-November, 2005 I received such and email. Boyd Green, the son of Bob Green, dropped me a line. Boyd wrote, "Michael, my father is having a book published that is a hunter's devotional. I don't know many people in the outdoor industry but he would like for someone of recognition to endorse his book and possibly write a foreword for it. You were the first one that came to my mind." Well, the first thought that came to my mind was, who could I ask to take part in this? I emailed Boyd back telling him that I would do whatever I could to help and gave him my phone number Bob could contact me and I'd see what I could do.

Standing in Little's Taxidermy in Cordele, GA my cell phone rang. It was Thanksgiving week and the Southern Backwoods crew and I were waiting out the rain so we could get back in the woods. Bob was calling me and we finally got the chance to talk for the first time. He explained to me what he was looking for and what I could do to help. To be honest I was hesitant at first. Not towards Bob, but towards myself. How could I be a part in a book that could possibly touch so many lives just like mine? How could I help in a battle for eternal life and aid in reaching so many outdoorsmen and women all over the country, and possibly the world?

My cell phone rang on a cool, windy November day. Bob was calling; he had gotten turned around from my "stellar" directions to our meeting place for lunch. I was lucky that day, my wife Beth was by my side to give him better directions to the restaurant we were at. God bless her!! Finally Beth and I had the pleasure of meeting Bob and truly getting an insight on what his intentions were with this awesome book, to save souls, one outdoors person at the time. Over the next couple of hours, Bob and I shared stories about hunting, family, our lives, and just opened our worlds up to each other and it hit me like a ton of bricks. God was allowing me to have a small part in yet another of his plans and through his messenger, Bob, another door was opened.

So it is with great pleasure, honor, and the utmost respect, I am proud to present to you the work of a great man, father, husband and servant of our Lord, *In God's Crosshairs,* by my friend, Bob Green.

Michael H. Lee
Host of *Southern Backwoods Adventures* television series

PREFACE

I have been a hunter since I was very young, and there is nothing more exciting than seeing an old bird dog on a point and the flushing of quail, or the whistle of wings of duck, doves, or geese overhead, or a beautiful buck or bull in the crosshairs of my rifle. There are tens of thousands and even millions of hunters out there who feel the same way I do. They are looking for something to add excitement and meaning to life. Too many of them immerse themselves in hunting, but after the last bird is picked or the trophy is hung on the wall, the excitement doesn't last and meaning slips away again. They come up empty, relationships suffer, and sometimes their families fall apart.

It is because they neglect the thing, or the One, who is the Author of real meaning. That Author keeps trying to get His "crosshairs" on us, but we, like the wary old buck, keep avoiding Him and hiding. He has the answers to all of the problems of life and can meet every need we have if we will just allow Him to do so.

In God's Crosshairs uses 366 Bible verses from the Old Testament (one for every day of the year), and blends them with real hunting and wildlife stories making them relevant to problems we face every day. The more we can know God's way and do it, the more we slip back into His sights and live meaningful lives that He intended for us, the more peace there is in our families, and the more successful we are in all we do.

I wish I had owned a copy of this book fifty years ago and could have avoided many of the mistakes I have made that damaged relationships and hindered my success. It would be good if every hunter or outdoorsman today had one to read. Since you are reading these words, you have access to one. Settle back each morning for a few minutes, read and think about the devotional for that day. By the time the end of the year comes, you will have changed. I promise. If you miss a day, don't get discouraged. Start with the current date and continue on. Soon you will begin to move into God's crosshairs.

Happy reading, and as I write, I will pray for blessings of God on every reader.

JANUARY 1

How It All Began

Genesis 1:1 "In the beginning, God created the heaven and the earth."

As I sit in my deer stand or wait in my blind for a dove to fly by, I can see all the beauty around me. Many colorful birds and other creatures fly, crawl, or meander by. The awesome sunrise or majestic sunset floods my mind with wonder. Where did it all come from? Was it all by chance? I think not. It would be as impossible as building a watch by putting all of the parts in a box and shaking them up. The first verse in the Bible says that God created everything.

I don't remember when I went on my very first hunting trip. It seems like I was born hunting. Just about everybody in my family loved to hunt, and my dad or brothers probably carried me before I could walk.

I am thankful that they did, because I can enjoy God's creation more. The world has not always existed. God created it out of love so that He would have people around.

Prayer: God, thank You that Your love was so great that You created us and everything there is for us to enjoy. Amen.

JANUARY 2

Misfires

Genesis 1:31 "And God saw everything that He had made, and behold, it was very good."

Riding down the road in my truck one day, I saw a coyote and jumped out to shoot him with my shotgun. I pulled the trigger and nothing happened. It didn't fire. Whether the old buckshot shell was too old or whether it was defective from the factory, I will never know.

There are "misfires" in life. Bad things often happen to some mighty good people. One of my sons-in-law was killed in a car wreck one month ago today. Children die, good people get cancer and on and on. I think my shell was good from the factory and went bad. God, too, only created good things. It breaks His heart when evil comes in and messes things up. For us to be truly free to love Him, He must allow this to be an imperfect world with people who are weak and fail.

Prayer: God, thank You that You only do good things. Help me to use the freedom You gave me to love unselfishly. Amen.

JANUARY 3

A Day of Rest

Genesis 2:2 "And on the seventh day God ended His work, and He rested on the seventh day."

I hunt and fish to get away from the pressures and hassle of life and enjoy the outdoors, but after I skin the deer or clean the fish, I am still not satisfied. My mind is rested, but I am still restless inside. Then, I remember even God rested, though He is never tired. Then, it clicks. He set the example for us. We need a day every week to rest, worship, and enjoy our family and God created that day of rest.

Prayer: Lord, a wise man once said, "We are restless until we find our rest in You." I want to spend more time at rest with You. Amen.

JANUARY 4

No Accident

Genesis 2:7 "And the Lord formed man of the dust of the ground and breathed into his nostrils the breath of life; and man became a soul."

Our son, Boyd, was a little fellow and just learning to deer hunt. I built him a stand up in an oak in a prime location. One wet morning, as he was trying to climb up, he slipped and skidded all the way down the side of the tree to the ground. He was skinned up a little but otherwise unhurt. It could have been much worse. Accidents do happen in the woods, and we just try to minimize the damage.

There is something that was no accident—the creation of people and the rest of nature. It takes a great deal more faith to believe that man evolved on his own over billions of years than it does to believe that there was an intelligent being called a Creator.

God made the first man from the dust of the earth—from nothing—and put a living soul in him. I would rather believe the Bible that has stood for thousands of years than some man's opinion. By the way, because of the discovery of DNA and other things, more and more scientists are abandoning evolution and talking about "intelligent design."

Prayer: Lord, I believe You created every good thing from scratch. Since You created me, Your Word also tells me how to live at peace with You and others. Help me to do that. Amen.

JANUARY 5

Building Memories

Genesis 2:24 "Therefore shall a man leave his father and mother and shall cleave unto his wife and they shall be one flesh."

A few years ago, my brothers and some friends and I camped at 10,000 feet in the snow near Aspen, Colorado to hunt elk. We will never forget that, but it only lasted a few days.

The most important thing to me, though, is my marriage of nearly forty years to Martha. I am looking right now at an old anniversary card she gave me that says, "Bob, you keep giving me reasons to love you more each day, and to look forward to a life shared with you." That is the way God intended it, one man and one woman for life. Now it hasn't been easy, and at times, I thought we wouldn't make it. Sometimes, we don't even like each other, but we intend to continue to build sweet memories as long as we both live. Hard times, with God's help, can strengthen a marriage. Never think separation or divorce.

Prayer: Father, thank You for my dear wife and her faithfulness to me. Help me to be more thoughtful, kind, and unselfish than ever before. Help me never think of her faults but only her good points. In Jesus' Name, Amen.

JANUARY 6

Watch Out For Snakes

Genesis 3:1 "Now the serpent was more subtle than any beast of the field."

A week or so ago, I was deer hunting and decided to go in the middle of the day to see if patterns had changed, so I got out of my stand before dark. As I walked across the woods and a food plot, to my surprise, a huge five-foot rattlesnake was stretched out in it in the middle of December. My hunting buddies and I constantly have reminded each other to watch out for snakes. A bite could ruin your whole day!

In the Bible, a snake tricked Eve and she disobeyed God. She also influenced her husband, Adam, to do the same thing. It hurt them for the rest of their lives.

Temptations are like snakes. We can be fooled by them and they can ruin our lives. Be cautious and avoid them. Their bite is deadly. We don't have to let temptation get to us. The Bible tells us that God gives the strength to overcome any of them.

Prayer: Lord, help me to identify the evil things in life that seem all right at first. Give me strength to avoid them like a snake. Amen.

JANUARY 7

Children Are Gifts From God

Genesis 4:1 "And Adam knew Eve his wife; and she conceived and bore Cain, and said I have gotten a man from the Lord."

I will never forget the first deer my son killed. I had placed him securely in a stand in the best location on the property. A little after daylight, I heard, "Bang, bang, bang." It sounded like a dove-shoot rather than a deer hunt. I climbed down and hurried to him. He was all smiles. He had two deer—a good-sized doe, and another one about the size of a German shepherd dog. That was a great experience for both of us. He has never forgotten it.

Martha and I tried to spend lots of precious time with our son and two daughters, Dawn and Pam, before they left to build their families. We wanted to steer them right and set a good example before them. We brought them up in the church. They, their spouses, and our grandchildren, Emily, Molly, Jordan, Peyton, and Bryn, are true blessings from the Lord. It is so good to see them living godly lives. So many children are neglected and mistreated. It is no wonder they grow up wild.

Prayer: Lord, help us to realize that our children are special and deserve our time, respect, and loving discipline. Help me to let them know that they are important and that they belong to You. Amen.

JANUARY 8

My Brother's Keeper

Genesis 4:9 "And the Lord said unto Cain, where is Abel thy brother? And he said, I know not. Am I my brother's keeper?"

Cain had killed his brother, Abel, because of jealousy. God had accepted Abel's offering rather than his because Abel gave of his first and best. A great deal of jealousy can exist between children. Parents can reduce it by not comparing them on how many birds they killed, who killed the biggest deer, etc. Children often try to "outdo" one another to get approval of parents. We should make every effort to help each child feel accepted as they are. Sometimes the jealousy continues throughout life. This grieves the Lord, for He expects children to love each other and wish each other well. We do have responsibilities to get along with our siblings.

That was a hard thing for me growing up as the baby in the family, with one brother eight years and another four years older. It is hard to feel good about yourself and others if you never win.

Prayer: Lord, help me to examine my relationship to my family and others to see if there is any ill will and strengthen me to make things right. Amen

JANUARY 9

Like God

Genesis 5:1 "In the day that God created man, in the likeness of God made He him."

Have you ever noticed that deer antlers have certain characteristics in a certain location? In one section of our county, the tines are turned in a little on one side on many bucks that are killed. I have never seen any like them anywhere else. I suppose it is genetics.

God has created people with his markings. We know we can't see God like we can people with flesh and bone. We are different from everything else God has created. We are like God because we have a soul that lives forever. We can think and reason like God can. The most important difference is that we can know right from wrong. Flip Wilson used to say, "The devil made me do it." No, no one makes us do wrong. We make choices. Not society, parents, circumstances, other people, or anything else is to blame for our attitudes and actions.

Prayer: Lord it is humbling to know that You created me in Your image. Help me to bend my will to be like Yours. Amen.

JANUARY 10

Bad to the Bone

Genesis 6:5 "And God saw that the wickedness of man was great in the earth, and that every imagination of the thoughts of his heart was only evil continually."

It is interesting to sit quietly in the woods and see the wonders of nature. One afternoon about dark as I sat in my tree stand, squirrels suddenly began to chatter and birds scattered here and there. It wasn't long before a bobcat came sneaking quietly out of the bushes and crouched ever lower. Then, he sprang with a powerful thrust of his back legs trying to catch a squirrel.

The bobcat was trying to find a meal to survive. The squirrel scampered away trying to survive as well. In the wild, only the strong survive. God allows that in animals, but condemns it in human beings since we are created in His image.

God destroyed all mankind because they were evil—bad to the bone—everyone but Noah and his family. He wants to place His Spirit in us and change us to be like Him and He will, if we let Him.

Prayer: Lord, sometimes my mind is just plain evil. Allow Your Spirit to enter me and change me to be like Jesus. In His Name, Amen.

JANUARY 11

Good Stewards

Genesis 6:19 "And of every living thing of all flesh, you shall bring two of every sort shalt thou bring into the ark, to keep them alive with thee."

A neighbor I grew up with never considered seasons, bag limits, or any other game law. He never bought deer licenses or tags and usually had killed more than the limit before the season opened. I have often complained about limits until I noticed quail and dove populations are way down. The old folks remember when the sky was filled with doves and I remember, myself, when fields had several coveys of quail.

God has entrusted man with the wildlife and other natural resources. He commanded Noah to protect them. We should support good game laws for that purpose and abide by them, or if a law is bad, we should lobby to change it. God will honor our obedience to Godly civil law and we had better, or soon we won't have anything to hunt.

Prayer: God, You have created so much wildlife for us to enjoy and have given us the awesome responsibility of taking care of it. Help us to be good stewards. In Jesus' Name, Amen

JANUARY 12

God Forgives

Genesis 9:6 "Whoso sheddeth man's blood, by man shall his blood be shed: for in the image of God made He man."

A young preacher, who was confined to a wheelchair, and his wife were deer hunting. For some unknown reason, her rifle went off and killed him, though she was some distance away. It was an accident and no charges were filed.

Life is precious to God, and He makes provision for justice for someone who willfully takes a human life—the death penalty. The sixth commandment says, "Thou shalt not kill." This applies to an individual murdering someone. God allows society to rid itself of those who do not value human life and would take one. God is merciful and forgives. That heartbroken wife will not be held accountable. Even guilty people who willfully break God's law and sincerely ask God's forgiveness will receive it, though they might still have to be punished under the law. Any wrong, no matter how bad, can be forgiven.

Prayer: Thank You, Lord, that there is forgiveness for the innocent and the guilty, because You love us.

JANUARY 13

Mighty Hunter

Genesis 10:9 "He (Nimrod) was a mighty hunter before the Lord."

My mother's side of the family loved to hunt and fish. They were doing one or the other if they were not working. Some were planning to go when they were working. Someone in the family should have been named "Nimrod."

Nimrod of the Bible was said to be a mighty hunter "before the Lord." I take that to mean that his hunting was approved by the Lord, because he hunted in a way that gave honor to the Lord. It could also mean that God saw everything Nimrod was doing.

Hunting, within itself, does not honor or dishonor the Lord. There are those who believe that killing an animal is wrong. If that is true, God would not have approved of Nimrod and Jesus would have been a vegetarian, but we know He ate fish and other meats. What does dishonor Him is when we kill just to kill and waste, or when we hunt when we should be doing something else, like going to church or spending adequate time with our spouse and family.

Prayer: Lord, You have created everything to glorify You. Help us to glorify and honor You as we enjoy it. In Jesus' Name, Amen.

JANUARY 14

First Things First

Genesis 11:4 "They said, Go to, let us build us a city, and a tower whose top may reach into heaven, and let us make us a name."

A deer-hunting club I know has a good rule. After their hunts, they divide the kill equally among all of the hunters so that everyone gets some. Some hunters take what they kill and offer none to anyone, even the owner. That is a bad policy and bad manners.

The people of Babel were like that—selfish. They did everything for themselves and even ignored God. Good men sometimes spend most of their time on themselves and leave out their wives, children, and God. They realize what they have done too late, when their children are grown up and out of control or when their wife leaves.

Our first priority must be God, second is spouse and family, and everything else is down the line. Joy comes when we put first things first.

Prayer: Lord, I admit that I neglect You and my family far too much. Help me get my priorities straight. In Jesus' Name, Amen.

JANUARY 15

Finding your Way

Genesis 12:1 "Now the Lord had said to Abram, Get thee out of thy country, and from thy kindred, and from your father's house, unto a land that I will show thee: and I will make of thee a great nation, and I will bless thee, and make thy name great."

Some friends and I hunted coons late one night and were in thick woods well after dark. I was supposed to be able to get us out because I was raised nearby. I got turned around and everywhere I looked it looked the same. After hours of wandering, we finally found our way out. I would have known what direction to take if only I had my compass.

Abraham needed a compass. God told him to "go forth to a land I will show you." Down deep, all of us are trying to find our way. What job should I take? Where should we live? There are those who would attempt to lead us—people, convenience, society, and our own impulses or "animal instinct." If we live by animal instincts, we will be like animals—greedy, rude, lawless, undisciplined, and out of control.

Follow God to find your way. The Bible, prayer, and caring Christian family and friends—in that order—can show us the way.

Prayer: Lord, I find myself making decisions I regret and sometimes not knowing what to do. Help me to learn to follow You. In Jesus' Name, Amen.

JANUARY 16

Making Choices

Genesis 13:12 "Abram dwelled in the land of Canaan, and Lot dwelled in the cities of the plain, and pitched his tent toward Sodom."

As a teenager, I would go home from school, take ole Cindy, my bird dog, and quail hunt until dark, if I had my homework done and I wasn't practicing football or something. There was a little head that stuck out into a field in front of our house, where I would usually find Cindy pointed. The choice of those birds to return to the same place got them into trouble regularly.

Choices can be good or bad. A man called Lot chose to live near Sodom, which was considered to be full of "wicked and sinners before the Lord exceedingly." People can avoid trouble by staying out of wrong places, away from the wrong people, and entertaining bad thoughts. Lot's choice cost him his wealth, wife, and well being. Ungodly choices bring destruction. Choices are not forced upon us, and we can freely make good or bad ones.

Prayer: Father, help me to make choices that would please You and not violate Your Word. In Jesus' Name, Amen.

JANUARY 17

Pleasing God

Genesis 15:6 "And he believed in the Lord; and He counted it to him for righteousness."

My wife's Uncle Tom, knowing I liked to hunt, offered to show me a place for opening day. He wasn't a deer hunter, and I was a little skeptical. We drove probably twenty miles and walked through the woods a little farther. There were plenty of tracks and the soybeans had not been gathered, so there was plenty of food and water nearby.

I didn't have a stand in those days, so I returned and built a platform on a fork hanging out over the field. The next morning was bitter cold, and it was a long way to drive, but I went and killed the largest eight point I ever saw that weighed over 200 pounds field dressed. How I got him in my bronco by myself even field dressed is another bloody story. My "faith" in Tom's judgment paid off.

Abram's faith in God paid off, too. He "believed God and He counted it to him for righteousness." How do we really please God? The Bible says, "Be ye therefore perfect," (Matthew 5:48) but as hard as we try, we fail. Abram not only "believed" with his mind but showed it by living obediently.

That's how we please Him. Believe in Jesus and attempt to live for Him.

Prayer: Lord, I am reminded how much I miss the mark every day. Thank You that it is not what I can do but my trust in You that counts. In Jesus' Name. Amen.

JANUARY 18

Doing It God's Way

Genesis 16:2 "And Sarai said unto Abram, Behold now, the Lord hath restrained me from bearing. I pray thee, go in unto my maid; it may be that I may obtain children by her."

There are many deer hunters who are unsuccessful because they climb out of their stand too early. They are frustrated because they see the rear ends of lots of deer and don't get a chance to shoot. A little more patience in the stand would bring better results, as it would have for Abram and Sarai.

God had made a promise to give them a child, but they gave up on God because she was beyond childbearing age and it had not happened. Well, Abram did sleep with the maid and fathered Ishmael. Later, Sarai did give birth to Isaac, and the boys and their descendents, the Arabs and the Jews, have been at war ever since.

Sometimes, when we don't get our way, we divorce, cheat on our income taxes, lie or break God's law in some other way. We are impatient, so "we buy things we don't need with money we don't have to impress people we don't like," as famed preacher Adrian Rogers once said. Never violate God's principles. It will catch up with you. Wait on the Lord.

Prayer: Lord, help me to wait on You to meet my needs and not let impatience cause me to sacrifice my principles and ruin my reputation. In Christ's Name, Amen.

JANUARY 19

Too Hard For God

Genesis 18:14 "Is anything too hard for the Lord?"

In the 1960's, deer were not very plentiful where we hunted, and I had gotten a doe but not a buck. Others had, and that put a great deal of pressure on me. One day, as the sun was setting, I prayed a very short prayer, "Lord, let me get a buck today." I promise you that within ten minutes, I heard the unmistakable sound of a deer running through the leaves. He was a four pointer and he stopped within ten yards of my stand and I got him.

Some may think it was a sheer coincidence, but I believe for some strange reason God answered my prayer. Can God answer prayer? Yes, He is the Creator and can do anything. Will He answer prayer? Yes, He will answer prayers of the obedient according to His will.

Abram was ninety-nine and had no legitimate son by Sarai, though God had promised one and it was the desire of their hearts. God miraculously gave them Isaac in their old age.

Do you think God is answering your prayers? He will, if you are faithful.

Prayer: Lord, sometimes I don't think You are listening and there are some prayers I really need answered. Give me what You want me to have. I turn it over to You. In Jesus' Name, Amen.

JANUARY 20

Never Look Back

Genesis 19:26 "But his wife looked back from behind him, and she became a pillar of salt."

As I sat in my deer stand in a tight fork one morning, a huge buck—eight points or better, with horns way outside his ears—came running by from my left. I eased my rifle to my right shoulder, and as I was taking aim, the fork caught me and I could swing no further. He got away and I was sick. It was the biggest one I had ever seen. I have thought of that many times and wondered, "What if?" You can't beat yourself up over stuff like that. You have to move on.

Lot's wife looked back, yearning for her belongings and past that had been destroyed, disobeyed God, and became a block of salt. We can't look at what might have been.

Prayer: Lord, Help me to only look back with joy or to make things right. Forgive me of my failures and help me to look to brighter days. In Jesus' Name, Amen.

JANUARY 21

Telling the Truth

Genesis 20:2 "And Abraham said of Sarah, his wife, She is my sister."

I was invited to a dove shoot several years ago. The limit was twelve and the possession limit was twenty-four. The doves covered us up and I kept shooting, as everyone else did. I finally left the field reluctantly with thirty-eight, though I had killed far more that I couldn't find. I felt really guilty and have never knowingly violated the law again. Though he did the same, the owner has never respected me in the same way, though I apologized. He had a different standard for me, the preacher.

Abraham lied about Sarah to protect his hide. Another man took his wife, and if God had not warned him in a dream, the man would have sinned by sleeping with Abram's wife.

We lie about "small things" like how many doves we killed or how big the fish was that we caught, and we cheat on our taxes and other things that are dishonest and deceitful. We are at a low point when we can't be trusted by our spouse, children, friends, co-workers, and even the law. God condemns it.

Prayer: God, help me to be trustworthy in my words and actions because I love You. In Jesus' Name, Amen.

JANUARY 22

Trusting God

Genesis 22:12 "Lay not thine hand upon the lad, neither do thou anything unto him for now I know that thou fearest God seeing thou hast not withheld thine only son from me."

Last year a deer hunter climbed into his tripod deer stand. One of the legs collapsed and he fell fifteen or so feet to the ground and was injured very seriously. He made the mistake of failing to examine it to see if it was reliable.

Abraham obeyed God and would have sacrificed his only son, Isaac. He was putting his total faith in God, not knowing what the result would be. God did not want him to kill his son but to show Abraham how strong Abraham's faith was.

Sometimes we fail to put our trust in God and live for Him, fearing that we will miss something or thinking that man's way is best. We are tested, like Abraham, to see if we believe God. Are you standing the test?

Prayer: Lord, help me know how to respond to the tests of lift and give me the will to trust You. In Jesus' Name, Amen.

JANUARY 23

Facing Life with Faith

Genesis 23:19 "And after this, Abraham buried Sarah his wife."

We might fish, hunt, or just get out in the woods to escape the pressures of life. There is nothing wrong with that in moderation, but sometimes we have to deal with the hardships of life in other healthy ways.

Abraham's life-long mate died and he had to buy a place and bury her. How hard that must have been! Our son and daughter-in-law, about three months along in her pregnancy, were alerted that the baby might have a dreadful genetic disorder in which the lungs never develop. It happened just like they said. Though the pregnancy went full-term, our little granddaughter, Bethany, was only with us fifteen days.

It was inspiring to see how our son and daughter-in-law, Boyd and Brooke, approached it in faith. They never blamed God, though they still deal with their grief. Their faith in Him is strong, and they will see Bethany again in Heaven.

We may not have to bury a spouse or child, but we will face hardship in life. It can depress us and keep us down or we can face life with faith.

Prayer: Lord, in those times, help us remember what the Bible says, "My grace is sufficient for you, for power comes through weakness." In Jesus' Name, Amen.

JANUARY 24

Selecting a Spouse

Genesis 24:37 "My master made me swear saying, Thou shalt not take a wife to my son of the daughters of the Canaanites, in whose land I dwell."

These days a great deal is being said about "gene pool" in upgrading deer herds. People harvest bucks with substandard characteristics to improve the stock. That, along with improving food and mineral sources, is a good idea.

Abraham knew the importance of selecting a good wife for his son, one who worshipped God and not idols like the Canaanites. My criterion was to select someone I would be proud of if I became president. Obviously, the wife we marry is the one we should stick with for life, but if we are choosing, the Scripture says not to be "unequally yoked." That means Christians should only date and marry Christians. A poor choice means nothing but trouble. If you are married and made a bad choice, pray for them and think of their good qualities. Don't be critical. Let God handle their faults.

Prayer: Help me to select the mate of Your choosing and be the best mate I can be to my spouse. In Christ's Name, Amen.

JANUARY 25

The Good Life

Genesis 25:8 "Abraham gave up the ghost, and died in a good old age."

Why did Abraham seem to be satisfied with his life? Was it because he killed the biggest deer, had the biggest four-wheel drive pickup, or spent lots of time in the woods?

When you get to the end of your life, will you be satisfied? Some people look back and call themselves a failure. What will really make us satisfied? First, if we trust Christ and know we are going to heaven, we don't have to be afraid. Next, if you have been obedient to God and lived for Him, you will be rewarded.

In the Bible, Jesus said that the person who "loses his life for my sake finds it." (Matthew 10:39) We can never be at peace by trying to get more things or have more fun. There is nothing wrong with things, unless they become gods, and there is nothing wrong with good clean fun, but if a person only lives for that, he will be disappointed. Abraham died happy because he lived a life of faith.

Prayer: Lord, thank You for making my life worthwhile. I know I have failed You and others many times, but You have made me complete. In Jesus' Name, Amen.

JANUARY 26

Being a Blessing

Genesis 26:4 "And in thy seed shall all the nations of the earth be blessed."

I haven't killed a deer in several years, though I have hunted faithfully. My son, daughter, and son-in-law have gotten several nice ones. It could be because they are better hunters, but I would rather believe it is location. I place them in the best places. I enjoy seeing them grin when they get one. My daddy used to say, "Boys, I'd rather see you catch a fish than catch one myself." It is thrilling to be a blessing to others.

God promised Abraham that he and his children would bless the whole earth. That has certainly been true through Jesus, the Son of God, whose earthly parent was a descendant of Abraham.

My wife and I have attempted to raise our children to bless others by taking them to church, teaching them to pray, and modeling the Christian life before them. The reason I write is to be a blessing to people I will never see.

Prayer: Lord, help me not just to live for myself and for here and now. Make me and my family a blessing to others. In Jesus' Name, Amen.

JANUARY 27

Honesty

Genesis 27:36 "Is not he rightly named Jacob, for he hath supplanted me these two times?"

A man holds a certain large buck record and was caught illegally hunting over bait. He is being investigated and his record may be taken away and it will always be tainted, even if they do not find him guilty.

Jacob plotted with his mother and deceived his blind and aging dad so that he gave his best blessings to Jacob rather than the rightful heir, Esau, the oldest. Jacob had to run for his life and was alienated from his family for over twenty years. He was known as a "trickster."

Families need to be able to believe and trust each other. Children hear dads laugh about trading someone a defective knife or gun deceitfully. The phone rings and mom says, "Tell them I'm not here." Children see parents tell the preacher, "We'll be there Sunday" and then not show up. They also observe their parents set the cruise control above the speed limit, intentionally breaking the law. All of this and the parents wonder why their children lie to them and become dishonest. Children tend to be what the parents model.

Prayer: Lord, help me to examine my habits to see what kind of things I am teaching others to do by the example I set. Am I honest? In Jesus' Name, Amen.

JANUARY 28

Gratefulness to God

Genesis 28:22 "And of all that thou shalt give me
I will surely give the tenth unto thee."

A number of years ago, I overheard a well-paid businessman bragging to his elderly parents about giving $500 to the church that year. I observed with interest that he was taking long, expensive hunting and fishing trips and buying expensive guns regularly. His giving impressed his parents, but it didn't impress God.

Jacob, out of gratitude for God's provision and protection, pledged to give ten percent of all God would give him. We are commanded to give that much and more today. What we have really is not ours. We might have earned it, but He gave us the ability, health, and opportunity to do so. Our gratefulness to God can be measured by how much we give back to Him.

Prayer: Giver of all I have, forgive me for my selfishness and teach me to give out of gratitude as I have received. Thank You. Amen.

JANUARY 29

Bearing Children

Genesis 30:1 "Rachael envied her sister and said to Jacob, give me children, or else I die."

I have noticed that some does have one fawn and others have two. I would guess that some have none, since you can see does without fawns in the spring, when they should have them.

Rachael blamed Jacob because she could not have children. Jews, in those days, felt that they were cursed if they had none. Some couples today cannot have children and become upset and depressed when they can't, though our culture doesn't feel that it is a disgrace. Men and women both sometimes feel that they are less than they should be when they can't conceive.

They should look at it more positively. Maybe the Lord allowed it so that they could help others with children or adopt. There are many unwanted children in America and across the world who need godly parents. There would be fewer abortions if more couples were ready to adopt. When one door closes, perhaps God is opening another.

Prayer: Father, whether we have children or not is in Your hands. Help us to trust You with that and seek Your will about ministering to someone else's children or adopting. In Jesus' Name, Amen.

JANUARY 30

Other Gods

Genesis 31:30 ". . . wherefore hast thou stolen my gods?"

This statement from Laban, Jacob's uncle, revealed that he served many gods. He owned small household figurines and probably had an altar where he bowed down to them.

We don't usually have idols of wood or stone like that, but we can put other things ahead of God. It may be self, job, hobby, things we own or want, family, or something else. Does it take you away from worship or keep you from serving the Lord? Hunting, fishing, or some other sport has become the god of many people. They are so wrapped up in it until they don't have time even for Almighty God.

It sets the stage for their children or others who are watching them to follow in their footsteps. They are accountable to God when they lead others astray. They may be leading them straight to hell.

Prayer: Dear God, please open my eyes to anything that I would put ahead of You. In Jesus' Name, Amen.

JANUARY 31

Mistreating a Spouse

Genesis 31:50 "If thou shalt afflict my daughters
. . . God is my witness between me and thee."

Laban had given two daughters to Jacob in marriage and warned him that if he mistreated them, God would be watching. Laban was right. As the popular song says, "God is watching from a distance." That is a great deal of comfort to those who love and obey God, but scary to those who are unbelievers.

The game warden is a threat to those who disobey the law. He helps preserve wildlife for our recreation and is a friend to most of us.

We have the same warning Jacob got. If we mistreat our spouse, we are under the watchful eye of God, who holds us accountable.

Prayer: Dear Father, thank you for watching over me and my family and for holding me accountable to take good care of them. In Jesus' Name, Amen.

FEBRUARY 1

Attitude Adjustment

Genesis 32:24 "And (Jacob) wrestled a man with him until the breaking of the day."

My wife and children bought me a new rifle and scope for Christmas one year. The first time I shot it, I got nowhere near the target. After lots of shooting and adjusting, it was finally pretty close.

Jacob knew he had to face his angry brother Esau that he had cheated twenty years before, so he prayed to God for protection. God answered the prayer by sending an angel to give Jacob an "attitude adjustment." They wrestled all night, and in the process, Jacob was a changed man.

Many times, settling conflicts with other people requires a change in me. Like my new rifle, I have to make adjustments so that I will be on target. "I'm sorry" and "excuse me," is not only for my wife and other people to say. I have to do it, too. A person who can't apologize is full of pride.

Prayer: Lord, adjust my thinking however You must when I am wrong, so that I can be at peace with others. In Jesus' Name, Amen.

FEBRUARY 2

An Altar to God

Genesis 33:20 "And he (Jacob) erected there an altar."

We are living in a very mobile society, and many families move a great deal. We have moved about a dozen times in the forty years we have been married. When we arrived at our new home, I immediately started looking for places to hunt or made plans to go back the short distance to my birthplace to old hunting spots.

Some families who move find places for shopping, recreation, etc., immediately but take months to find a place to worship and sometimes never find one. What a shame! There are families who have family altars at home, read the Bible, and pray together, but others don't.

One of the first things Jacob did when he got back home was build an altar of worship. He was blessed of God because he put Him first. Jesus said, "Seek ye first the kingdom of God and His righteousness and all these things shall be added unto you." (Matthew 6:33)

Prayer: Lord, give me the desire to make worship my first priority. In Jesus' Name, Amen.

FEBRUARY 3

Tarnishing What's Pure

Genesis 34:2 ". . . he took her and lay with her and defiled her."

One opening day of deer season, an excited hunter walked to his stand on his own land where he had scouted and found lots of tracks and other deer sign, only to find another hunter sitting up in it! The whole day was tainted, for his hope of getting that big one was diminished. Since opening day is usually the best day of the year, the whole season was damaged.

In the Bible story, Dinah, a young Jewish virgin, was raped or "defiled," which meant she was no longer pure. This was a serious matter that caused a war between the families involved and ruined her hopes of getting married and having children.

When sex outside marriage occurs, the man and woman are tainted. A future mate might wonder if the person could be trusted. Each party bears the guilt and shame of such a relationship all of their lives. If a woman is raped, obviously, she bears no guilt. Though God can and does forgive people who ask for forgiveness and forsake their sin, something called purity is tarnished and can never be recovered.

Prayer: Lord, help me to treasure what is pure and help me to be faithful before and after marriage. In Jesus' Name, Amen.

FEBRUARY 4

Tattling

Genesis 37:2 "Joseph brought his father their evil report."

In some families, there is a great deal of competition to the point of jealousy over hunting and many other things. Children sometimes battle hard to get the attention of parents and others. They often feel they can get closer to certain people by giving bad information about the competition, which might be a brother or sister. Parents should discourage this tattling. When Joseph did it, his brothers became very angry and they later sold him into slavery.

Some competition is healthy, but children should never feel that they have to compete for the love and attention of their parents. This can be avoided by telling them you love them and hugging them often, spending time with them, and giving honest praise for good qualities, but never comparing them to each other. One may make good grades and another may be a good athlete. Make them both feel proud. Discipline appropriately but never when you are angry. Teach them to compliment each other.

Prayer: Lord, I might be guilty of giving bad reports about others. Help me to look for the good in others and to teach my children to do the same. In Jesus' Name, Amen.

FEBRUARY 5

Treating Children Fairly

Genesis 37:4 "And when his brethren saw that their father loved him (Joseph) more . . . they hated him."

My brothers, James and Bill, are eight and four years older than I am. When we were children, sometimes Daddy took them hunting at night and wouldn't let me go. He said I was too young, and he was right, but I didn't understand that then. I thought it was very unfair and that he loved them better. One preacher has said, "Children are keen observers but poor interpreters."

Joseph's brothers had a valid complaint. Jacob gave him a special coat and other favors and did play favorites. Joseph was born by Jacob's favorite wife and she had died, but that was no reason to mistreat the other children.

Children of different ages, personalities, and needs cannot always be treated equally, but they should be treated fairly. This has to be explained very carefully at the time. Favoritism can be detected by children and different treatment is sometimes misinterpreted. They must know we love them equally.

Prayer: Lord, help us to know that You love us equally and help us to be fair with our children. In His Name, Amen.

FEBRUARY 6

Dealing With Adversity

Genesis 37:28 "They sold Joseph to the Ishmeelites for twenty pieces of silver."

Daddy told a story of a man who climbed a tree to find out what the coon dogs had treed. They were at the foot of the tree barking and clawing the bark off, when the man slipped and tumbled through the darkness hitting every limb on the way down until he hit the bushes. The dogs immediately pounced on him and he had to be rescued by the other hunters. That is adversity.

Joseph had been sold into slavery by his brothers into Egypt, which was a long way from family and friends. He was less than twenty years old. Nevertheless, he maintained his strong character in spite of temptations, false accusations, and even imprisonment.

Character is what we are when we think no one is looking. It is trusting God, not panicking, and believing that somehow good is going to come of it. That is also called "faith," and that is how you deal with adversity. Don't compromise honesty, morality, or attitude though things look bad. The Bible says, "All things work together for good to those who love God, to them who are the called according to His purpose." (Romans 8:28)

Prayer: Father, help me in those times when the chips are down so that I will not compromise. In Jesus' Name, Amen.

FEBRUARY 7

Moral Temptation

Genesis 39:10 "He (Joseph) hearkened not unto her to lie by her or to be with her."

Most animals in the wild breed any other animal of their specie they come into contact with that is ready. There are some exceptions. I understand that wild geese have a mate for life. Bucks and most other animals fight for dominance and attract as many partners as possible. We have come to that point in America, where most men and even women now feel the same way. Some people don't bother to get married. They just "shack up" with no apparent conscience about it at all.

Joseph was young, away from home, and unmarried. Nobody would know if he yielded to the temptation of Potipher's wife. Joseph's reply to her was, "How can I do this great wickedness and sin against God?" Though nobody else might ever know, Joseph knew that God, the Righteous Judge, would.

God's plan is that sex be between one man and one woman married to each other for life. Anything else is sin. When temptation comes, take Joseph's advice and run.

Prayer: Lord, help me to recognize and avoid the deadly temptation of sexual sin. In the Name of Jesus, Amen.

FEBRUARY 8

The Real Source of Wisdom

Genesis 40:8 "Do not interpretations belong to God?"

Sportsmen I know subscribe to magazines and try to keep up with the latest methods of hunting and fishing. It is sort of a Bible to them. Some of the advice comes from people in distant states and might not apply in our area. We really need to get our information closer to home from more reliable sources.

Servants came to Joseph for advice, and he knew where to go for wisdom—to God. He gave God the credit. Joseph interpreted their dreams, and they turned out just like Joseph said they would.

True wisdom only comes from God. His children who are close to Him through obedience, Bible study, and prayer can get practical wisdom for everyday life. He will lead them to good decisions about jobs, a spouse, business, and anything else. There is no need to be in doubt about things you can learn in the Bible, like moral issues. We must obey what we know to be right, and God will lead us on other things.

Prayer: Lord, I need to make smart decisions, and they come from listening to You through prayer, Your Word, and other Christians. Help me know and follow Your wisdom. In Jesus' Name, Amen.

FEBRUARY 9

God's Purpose in Life

Genesis 41:41 "And Pharaoh said unto Joseph, see, I have set thee over all the land of Egypt."

Sometimes we get confused about what life is all about. As much as I love it, hunting and fishing is not what we are here for. There is nothing fundamentally wrong with it, you understand. However, you can kill all the game and catch all of the fish and it doesn't really satisfy you down deep.

After Pharaoh saw God at work in Joseph, he put him over all of Egypt. The purpose of that was to save the Jewish people and the world from seven years of dry weather that would have starved them to death.

We won't all be kings or rich and famous, but we are here for a purpose and we are not here by accident. God will work His purpose in us if we are willing to be used. That is where life's blessings really are.

Prayer: God, we thank you that you care about us enough to make our lives worthwhile. Don't let us be satisfied with a life with no purpose. In Jesus' Name, Amen.

FEBRUARY 10

Justice Wins in the End

Genesis 42:6 "And Joseph's brethren came and bowed down themselves before him with their faces to the earth."

Sometimes even Christian hunters compromise their principles, break the law, or stretch the truth to make themselves look better than someone else. They estimate high on how long the tines were or how much the deer weighed or how long the shot was. It is hard to play by the rules and simply tell the truth at times, isn't it? Wouldn't you rather be known for your integrity than for being an outstanding sportsman?

Joseph's brothers had sold him into slavery, and in the end they had to bow down to him. That happens so many times. The person we have mistreated sometimes becomes the boss. We know that God's justice will come out on top. It doesn't seem like it ever will. Evil people seem to make more money, get the good jobs, and become the most popular. Good will win. Psalm 37:9 says, " . . . evildoers will be cut off, but those who wait upon the Lord, they shall inherit the earth."

Prayer: Lord, help me to realize that I can be a person of integrity and still win. I want Your approval of me rather than other hunters' approval! In Jesus' Name, Amen.

FEBRUARY 11

Admitting Guilt

Genesis 42:21 "We are verily guilty concerning our brother, in that we saw the anguish of his soul, when he besought us, and we would not hear him; therefore is this distress come upon us."

One serious and glaring flaw in men, and really in most people, is that we think it is weak to admit we are wrong and say, "I'm sorry." We try to shift the blame to our spouse or someone else. I guess we are trying to make others believe we are perfect for fear that someone might laugh at us or look down on us. That is pride, and the Bible says that God hates pride and that pride comes before the fall.

Most of the time, we have to be backed into a corner before we admit we are wrong. The brothers remembered how they treated Joseph only after they got into a bind. Lots of marriages could be saved if we would admit it when we are wrong. What do we have to prove by denying the truth? There is a quality of Jesus present when a person will humble himself no matter what it might cost him.

Prayer: Lord, make me honest enough to know when I am wrong and admit it. In Jesus' Name, Amen.

FEBRUARY 12

Chickens Come Home to Roost

Genesis 45:3 "And his brethren could not answer him, for they were troubled at his presence."

Normally, you would think that if brothers were reunited after many years, it would be a happy time, but that was not the case here. They thought Joseph would get revenge.

As a boy, I heard of people going to robin roosts at night "thrashing." The birds would light in the same trees every night by the hundreds, and you could go there with sticks and kill as many as you wanted to eat. They, like chickens, came home to roost.

Joseph's brothers mistreated him, thinking they would get by with it but they didn't. It came back to haunt them, and Joseph had the power to end their lives. The Bible tells us that we have to give an account for "every idle word." We may seem to get by with a great deal of evil because God is gracious and patient. Most of the time, we have to face up to the bad things we do before we die, and Jesus says there will be a time when what has been whispered will be shouted from the housetop.

Prayer: Dear Lord, I know that You know everything I do and I have to give account. Help me to live with that in mind. In Jesus' Name, Amen.

FEBRUARY 13

Counting Your Blessings

Genesis 47:9 "And Jacob said unto Pharaoh, the days of my pilgrimage are an hundred and thirty years; few and evil have the days of the years of my life been."

My cousin, Sam, and I were probably five or six years old and decided we would go hunting while our mothers weren't looking. As I was messing with the .22 rifle, it fired off and shot in the bank of the ditch right beside him. It is a miracle that it didn't hit him.

Jacob was nearing the end of his life filled with pessimism, though he had been blessed. He had lived all those years with no mention of sickness and twelve sons with plenty of material goods. Joseph had been found alive and was a ruler in Egypt. There was no reason to be negative, for he had truly been blessed, as Sam and I were when the bullet missed.

It is easy to fall into the trap of negativism and look at what we don't have rather than what we do have. It is just as easy to be thankful. People would rather hear us count our blessings rather than lament all of the time. We dishonor our Maker when we forget how he has blessed us. Think a minute. Haven't you been blessed lately?

Prayer: Lord, I have everything I need because I have You, a family, and plenty of other blessings. Thank You, Amen.

FEBRUARY 14

The Old Home Place

Genesis 47:30 "But I will lie with my fathers and thou shalt carry me out of Egypt and bury me in their burying place."

I have been privileged to go to some far away places to hunt. Those trips were memorable and will always be special times, but they will never be as special as hunting with family on the old home place. There were no deer in those days in our parts, but we hunted squirrels, robins, ducks, and quail aplenty. Covering that old place with my brothers was really special.

Unlike Israel, I have no desire to be buried there, necessarily. My wife and I have grave plots in her hometown. However, I enjoy returning to the home place as my two brothers, James and Bill, did recently. Those memories are dwarfed by the ones Martha, my wife, and our children have accumulated, but they are still there.

Like Israel, we have to make plans for the end of life. Things like taking care of our spouse after we die and where we will be buried are important, but what becomes of us after we die is crucial. We determine whether we go to heaven or not before we die by putting our trust in Jesus.

Prayer: Dear Lord, help me to prepare myself for the future by placing my faith in You now. In Jesus' Name, Amen.

FEBRUARY 15

Blessing Children

Genesis 49:1 "Gather yourselves together that I may tell you that which shall befall you in the last days."

Jacob was at the end of his life and gathered his children around him to review their behavior and forecast what they would do in the future. His predictions were based on past behavior, but a bad past can be overcome.

I bought a bird dog puppy from very famous blood lines and took him to one dog trainer who said, "The dog is gun shy and cannot be trained." I took him to another one and after a few weeks he said, "Somebody has mistreated the dog. He's not gun shy. He just needs a little time."

Children are not destined from birth to be good or bad. They have a sin nature, but they need time with their parents, who need to praise them, tell them they love them, expect good things from them, and consistently, firmly discipline them when they willfully disobey. Bless them by bringing out their best traits and giving them encouragement. They must know that parents are on their side. Teach them and involve them in your activities. They will never forget it.

Prayer: Dear Lord, You gave us our children. Help us to bless them by our words and actions, so their future will be bright. In Jesus' Name, Amen.

FEBRUARY 16

This Too Shall Pass

Genesis 50:4 "And when the days of his mourning were past . . ."

Hunters were out quail hunting one day and a bird flushed and never got very high off the ground. An inexperienced hunter shot at the bird and accidentally killed another hunter's high priced dog that he loved. The owner became angry and has never gotten over it to this day. The two men who were close friends hardly speak to each other now.

Tough times are going to come in all of our lives no matter who we are. Family members have diseases and accidents and die–parents, spouses, children, as well as close friends. People lose their jobs, divorce, and their children get into trouble. Losing a dog is one of the more trivial loses in life.

It is normal to have all kinds of emotions about such things, but we do not have to "grieve as those who have no hope." The Christian attitude is to accept things, face them, put them behind us, and then turn them over to God. We never get over these things completely, but we can look ahead in hope. There is heaven to look forward to, a better day for those who obey the Lord, and comfort for those who put their faith in Jesus.

Prayer: Heavenly Father, I cannot bear the tough times in life alone. Help me put my trust in You. In Your Name, Amen.

FEBRUARY 17

Handling Change

Exodus 1:8 "There arose a new king over Egypt, which knew not Joseph."

Years ago in our community, when we wanted to go hunting, we didn't have to ask neighbors if we could hunt on their land. You just gave them some of the game and you really didn't have to do that. Things have changed these days. I saw some ducks flying into a neighbor's pond one cold day near my house in the country, so I ran got my shotgun and shot some. I was wrong and it offended the neighbor. I had to apologize.

Things do change and we do have to accept it humbly and adjust. A new boss, changes in the law, children leaving home, higher prices, and diminished hunting lands all require change. God gives us the ability to adjust to all changes by having a humble attitude and sensitivity toward others

The children of Israel had to adjust to the new king and his bad attitude toward them. God finally relieved their problem by moving them into the land of Canaan. Be patient and wait on the Lord. He will meet all of your needs, too.

Prayer: Dear Lord, when Joseph died, the Egyptians treated his people badly. Help me have a Christian attitude when things change for the worse. I wait on you. Amen.

FEBRUARY 18

Caring About Others

Exodus 2:11 "When Moses was grown, he went out unto his brethren, and looked on their burdens."

Outdoorsmen have a reputation for being hardhearted and not caring for anybody but themselves. Some of us think it is "macho" to be like that. We forget our anniversaries and other special dates and forget commitments we have made to our children and others. We get so involved in what we like to do to the point that we overlook the needs of others. Sportsmen are not the only ones who do that. If "self" is at the center, we just focus on what pleases us and gives us our "strokes." In some families, when deer hunting season starts, the family is on hold until it is over.

Moses saw that his people were mistreated slaves. He took it to an extreme when he killed an Egyptian to defend an Israelite. God used his caring attitude to free Israel later on.

There are "takers" in life and others who care enough to meet needs of others. God is a giver. The Bible says, "For God so loved the world, He gave . . ." (John 3:16)

Prayer: God help me to give like You and to think more about others and less of myself. In Jesus' Name, Amen.

FEBRUARY 19

Fearing God

Exodus 1:17 "But the midwives feared God and did not as the king of Egypt commanded them but saved the man children alive."

The king had become fearful that Israel had become too large and would overthrow him, so he commanded the Egyptian midwives to kill all of the male children. They, rightfully, put the law of God above the king's and would not obey. God blessed them for it.

The Bible teaches us that we should submit to rulers because of their appointment by God, even though they might be overbearing and brutal. It also teaches that we must "obey God rather than man." The Apostles in the New Testament would not obey when they were told not to preach about Jesus.

The midwives feared God. People willfully do things they know are wrong, indicating they do not fear God. When we go into the woods, we know to look out for snakes, packs of coyotes, and anything that might be rabid. They can kill you. By the same token, we should fear God even more and want to obey Him, because He controls what happens to us beyond death and forever.

Prayer: Dear Lord, help me to fear You so much that I obey, knowing that when I do, I have nothing to fear. In Jesus' Name, Amen.

FEBRUARY 20

My Salvation

Exodus 15:2 "The Lord is my strength and song and He is become my salvation."

A friend and I were hunting elk in unfamiliar territory in Montana. He and I had gone in different directions looking for tracks. Suddenly, a white out snowstorm came over the mountain blowing horizontally. I got under the low limbs of an evergreen and was safe there, but suddenly realized the roads were covered and we had only a day's supply of food. My fears were unfounded because the snow soon stopped, and my friend found our way out, though we could hardly see the road.

The Scripture above is the song of Moses after God delivered them out of Egypt by parting the Red Sea. God had saved them from their enemies.

You may be going through trying times in your work, marriage, finances, health, or some other crisis in life, and you may be wondering where to turn. There may be friends, family, ministers, or others who can help. They will usually disappoint us, because they cannot fix our problem completely. Turn to the Lord. Deepen your commitment. Read His Word, pray, and adjust your living so that you live by His principles. Abandon any known sin in your life and make sure you worship regularly. He is your answer.

Prayer: Lord, I am lost without you. Save me. In Your Name, Amen.

FEBRUARY 21

Forever

Exodus 15:18 "The Lord shall reign forever and ever."

Once I spent several days in the home of an avid hunter while I spoke in churches nearby. All the way around his huge balcony overhanging the den, he had maybe twenty-five trophy buck mounts, one of which measured 180 or so on the Boone and Crocket scale. It was third in the state of Georgia at one time but is far down the list now. The number one buck will be replaced in the future.

In a world where things are always changing and no one is on top forever, it is good to know something is permanent. The Lord will reign forever. That should tell us where to put our trust. There is nothing basically wrong with hunting for big bucks as long as we know that compared to serving the Lord, it is not important at all!

Prayer: Lord, help me to love You above all, because You are forever. In Jesus' Name, Amen.

FEBRUARY 22

Destructive Complaining

Exodus 16:2 "And the whole congregation of the children of Israel murmured against Moses and Aaron in the wilderness."

God had used Moses and Aaron to lead Israel out of Egypt, and now they were criticizing them and complaining that things weren't like they used to be.

An old gentleman in his nineties had been in a hunting club for many years. He was now almost blind, but the other members would take him out in the woods and set him in a chair with another hunter at a safe distance. Things were not the same as they used to be, and he let deer slip by sometimes, but he never complained about his health and always had a good attitude. Everyone loved the old man and enjoyed being around him.

People hate to be around negative people who are always complaining or criticizing someone. I like to be around folks who are positive, and I believe it honors the Lord. It communicates thankfulness.

Prayer: Lord, help me to have a positive, helpful, uncritical attitude toward leaders and reflect the spirit of Christ. In His Name, Amen.

FEBRUARY 23

He Meets Our Needs

Genesis 16:13 "And it came to past that at even the quails came up and covered the camp and in the morning the dew lay round about the host . . ."

Quail population is so low in Southeast Georgia that it is rare to find a covey of wild birds anymore. A hunter with a good dog could go out and find several a day about thirty years ago.

It was different with Israel. They were living off something called "manna" that God had provided six nights a week, and I am sure they were tired of having it for every meal. The Lord listened to the complaint of the people and added quail to their diet. I would like to have that answer to prayer today. It shows His great compassion.

God meets our needs even today. He has never promised to give us everything we want. Materialism and greed indicate that we love things more than we love Him. The wonderful thing is that He meets the needs of His obedient children that they don't even know they have. When He does, it brings real joy and satisfies the soul.

Prayer: Lord, thank You for providing our health, favorable weather, and opportunities to meet physical needs and for blessings we cannot imagine. Thank You. Amen

FEBRUARY 24

A Day of Rest

Genesis 16:29 "See, for the Lord hath given you the Sabbath, therefore He giveth you on the sixth day the bread of two days."

When the children of Israel gathered more than one day's supply of manna, it spoiled, except on the day before the Sabbath. He wanted them to keep the day holy—that is, different—and said so in other Bible verses. It is a day set aside for Him.

He still wants us to honor it today by using it as a day of worship and rest. We need it. Our bodies are not designed to go seven days a week. I believe hypertension, heart attacks, and other ailments are because we stress ourselves to the limit. God loves us and has provided the Sabbath for our good. Also, we cannot count on the blessings of God if we do not obey His Word. It is a matter of trust. He will bless our families, our work will get done, and we will have enough recreation if we simply follow His guidelines and find other times to do it except on His day!

Prayer: Dear Lord, You made us and care for us like You did Israel. Help us to trust You enough to honor Your day and look for Your blessings. In Jesus' Name, Amen.

FEBRUARY 25

Teamwork

Exodus 17:12 "Aaron and Hur stayed up his hands."

My son, Boyd, tells me about a video he saw in which a very large buck in the woods was confronted by a coyote. The buck turned in a different direction and another coyote appeared. The two of them together were able to bring the deer down and have a good meal, whereas, neither of them could have done it alone.

As Israel, led by Joshua, battled the army of Amalek, Moses stood on a hill watching the battle. When he held his hands up to God, they won, and when his hands were down, they lost. Moses got tired, but Aaron and Hur held up his hands and Israel won the battle.

Unity is important in businesses, churches, and especially families. Families should realize that they can accomplish more by communicating and agreeing on plans and working together. They need to support and help each other. Working and playing together is a good time to get to know each other better and build a tight bond. They need to be unselfish and do things others enjoy or need help with.

Prayer: Too often, Lord, families go their separate ways. Draw ours closer together and help me lead them to do so. In Jesus' Name, Amen.

FEBRUARY 26

Getting Things Done

Exodus 18:21 ". . . place such over them, to be rulers of thousands, and rulers of hundreds . . ."

Moses attempted to alone be the judge over perhaps a million people. Jethro, his father-in-law, saw him working all day and part of the night and not getting it all done. His advice was to train able men and divide up the work. That way, Moses would not burn out, and the people would be happier. That is good advice.

The old saying, "If you want anything done right, you'd better do it yourself," will kill you. We take a team approach to hunting. From planting the food plots, to buying the seed, to plowing the ground, to cleaning what we kill, we work together. Everyone feels that they belong, and things get done sooner and better.

Churches can learn from this. Pastors are the world's worst about failing to involve the whole congregation in the work. On the job, at church, or at play, involve the people. At home, have the children play a vital role in housekeeping or other work around the house. It will help them mature, get more work done, and help them feel good about themselves. That is not imposing on them. After all, they should feel responsible to help.

Prayer: Lord, help me to multiply myself by helping others get involved. In Jesus' Name, Amen.

FEBRUARY 27

A Kingdom of Priests

Exodus 19:6 "And ye shall be unto me a kingdom of priests."

Every fall, bucks begin to spar and sometimes fight to the death to be the dominant buck. Each one wants to "run the whole show." That is God's order to maintain deer population with the strongest ones reproducing.

God does not carry on His work that way with us. Though there are pastors, elders, deacons, bishops, etc., every Christian is a priest who is responsible to represent God to the people and speak to God for them. No one else can do for us what He has called us to do. We are all gifted to serve.

It is a true saying that you may be the only Jesus some people will ever see. Do others see Jesus in what you do? Do they hear about Jesus through what you say? Do they see Him in your attitude?

Prayer: Dear Lord, examine me and help me see if I am a true priest. In Jesus' Name, Amen.

FEBRUARY 28

God Answers

Exodus 19:19 "Moses spake, and God answered him by a voice."

Turkey hunting is a fascinating sport. The challenge is using a turkey caller and getting a gobbler in gun range. Sometimes you call, but there is no answer, even though he has heard, knows where you are, and will be there soon. Some answer and don't come, while others do.

Moses spoke to God, and He answered in an audible voice. God always answers, but I have never heard Him out loud. He doesn't always give us what we want. He may answer yes, no, or wait. He will always give His obedient children what we need and is never late in doing so.

If we want our prayers answered, our lives must be full of prayer, worship, faith, right relationships with others, obedience, and purity. Is He not answering your prayers? He might have answered in a way you did not expect and you didn't recognize it, or you might not be walking close enough. A part of faith is that we have to trust Him with the answers.

Prayer: God, I know You answer our prayers in the best way possible. I trust You with them. In Jesus' Name, Amen.

FEBRUARY 29

First Place

Exodus 20:3 "Thou shalt have no other Gods before me."

Thanksgiving and Christmas are my favorite hunting times. Almost everything is in season and some family is usually around to hunt. When the children and grandchildren are around, we drop most of our hunting and shopping to be with them. That's all about priorities. I would rather be with family than hunt, if I can't do both. Now that is a big change for me, but it is true.

God says we have a choice between Him and other things that compete for our time, resources, and attention. What we choose rather than worshiping and obeying God is really our god, no matter what we say. Jesus said, "You cannot serve God and mammon (money)." (Matthew 6:24) He gives us free choice, but the choice of some other god will destroy us and our children. It could be money, power, position, sports, a truck, a rifle, or some person.

Prayer: Lord, You are my God. Help me to show that by the way I live and the choices I make. In Your Name, Amen.

MARCH 1

Influencing Others

Exodus 20:5 "I am a jealous God, visiting the iniquity of the fathers upon the children unto the third and fourth generation."

We are making some changes in land use to try to increase quail population. Control burning, thinning pines, and food plots are some things we do because habitat is important. Biologists tell us that birds will be healthier and numbers will be greater if the food supply is improved and there is shelter for protection from predators.

"Habitat," or the environment in which our children are raised, will affect them and their children and grandchildren. God said that if we worship other gods and live ungodly lives, the same thing will happen to our children. The old saying is true that an acorn does not fall far from the tree. Our children pick up our habits, language, and characteristics for better or worse.

As we traveled in Europe a few years ago, we were constantly confronted by children who would pick our pockets. We were shocked to learn that it was a way of life for a certain group of people. There were entire villages that lived on tourists, adults and children alike. The children knew no better, because that was what they were taught.

We are influencing our children and others every day. What we do or do not do will give others approval to do the same things. People are watching you.

Prayer: Dear Father, show me the changes I need to make to be the right kind of influence on others. In Jesus' Name, Amen.

MARCH 2

God's Name

Exodus 20:17 "Thou shalt not take the name of the Lord thy God in vain."

I have been invited to some hunts, wild game suppers, etc., where I have ended up embarrassed to be there. All of the gossiping, profanity, and other things were highly offensive. Even people who claim to be Christian set a bad example by drinking and misusing the name of our Lord. Athletes and movie stars sometimes give glowing testimonies about Christ and wear big crosses around their neck, but soon, you hear that they are living a Godless life! That is "using the Lord's name in vain." You don't have to be "cussing" to do it—just being a hypocrite.

There was an old cartoon where a wolf would go into the flock dressed up like a sheep. The shepherd dog worried with it all through the movie, but at the end, the sheep took off their disguises and they were all wolves. The sheep had all gradually been eaten up, because the dog was not on guard all the time. Taking God's name in vain is like that. If we are not careful, committed Christians can slip back in to dishonoring Him with their words and actions. Then, the first thing you know, others are doing the same thing.

God's Name should never be used, except with attitude of worship and we should never do or say anything, as a Christian, that would encourage others to say, "See there, Christians are no different from anyone else."

Prayer: Lord, You are holy and worthy of all respect and honor. Help me to choke before I would use Your Name with disrespect or sin and discredit You. In Jesus' Name, Amen.

MARCH 3

Honoring Parents

Exodus 20:12 "Honor thy father and thy mother that your days may be long."

In training bird dogs, it is crucial that they are taught to "honor" another dog's point. If they don't, another dog may have found a covey and he might rush on in and run up the birds before the hunter gets there. It is a hard thing to train them to do, because, if they don't smell the birds or see them on the ground, they usually won't stop.

God teaches us to honor our parents by obeying them while we are children and respecting them always. Parents have been through life and can help children avoid bad mistakes. Many a child has ruined their life by ignoring advice. When a child grows up, he has to make his own decisions, but it is still wise to at least consider his parents' advice. We should honor our parents always. When they are old, we should care for them and treat them with respect. It might mean we can take care of them in our home, or it might be medically the best thing to put them in an institution. They will always need our presence, love, and respect until the end. That is what family is all about.

Prayer: Lord, thank You for the parents I have and help me to honor them. In Jesus' Name, Amen.

MARCH 4

Sacredness of Life

Exodus 20:13 "Thou shalt not kill."

There are those who object to hunting but care less about human life. Protesters attempt to ban guns of all types and disallow hunting on public lands. The next step would be to outlaw it on private land. God put man over the other creatures and commanded us to be good stewards but did not speak against killing animals for food. Animals are lower than people.

All human life is sacred. An individual has no right to take the life of another human being. That is murder, and the Hebrew word here is talking about that. The Bible recognizes the need for governments to take the life of criminals for serious crimes. It also allows killing in wars to protect society and freedom. Taking a life because someone is seriously ill or disabled sounds like Nazism during World War II. God, not man, must determine "quality of life." Taking the life of an unborn baby is murder, because life begins at conception. Both of these issues arise only because of the selfishness of men. We feel that if someone inconveniences us, we can simply get rid of them. We should defend the right to life of the unborn and disabled.

Suicide is also against God's will for the same reason. Man should not decide if he lives or dies—only God. Some teach that if someone commits suicide, they go to hell. That is not so, we are saved by grace, and a person could get so depressed that they take their own life. That does not undo the work of grace. Only those who die without Jesus Christ go to hell.

Prayer: God, You are the Creator of all life, so may we value the unborn and disabled as we would all human life. For Jesus' sake, Amen.

MARCH 5

Adulteru

Exodus 20:14 "Thou shalt not commit adultery."

This is the downfall of this generation. Sex is one of the gods today that is destroying families of Christians and unbelievers alike. You can see the turmoil in the animal kingdom when sex has no rules and is left unchecked. Almost every species of male goes to war during the mating season to see who dominates. God set rules for intelligent beings to rise above that, but we often don't.

God created lifetime marriage for one man and one woman. Sex out side of marriage is sin, always. Jesus says that if a man "lusts," that is, if he or she cultivates a desire to get involved with someone other than his spouse, he commits adultery. Paul says that sexual sin is more serious than any other sin, because it is a sin against the body. If a person divorces and marries again, they are adulterous.

God created sex to carry on life and for enjoyment in marriage. If we violate it, families and little children are harmed.

Prayer: Lord, marriage is sacred. Help me be true to my spouse in every way "until death do us part." In Your Name, Amen.

MARCH 6

Stealing

Exodus 20:15 "Thou shalt not steal."

This is another of the Ten Commandments that God gave us to keep order in society and set moral standards. They are not the "ten suggestions." This one gives us the right to private property. Can you imagine how life would be if I could take what you had, when I wanted to, without punishment? It would be chaos.

As we have camped and hunted, we never have been concerned about letting guns, money, or other possessions lie out in the open. You hear stories about things disappearing from camps now. Whether they were stolen or misplaced by the owner is not known. We assume somebody took it.

It is sad that a thing like that would even pass through someone's mind. Unfortunately, it is a logical conclusion. When we were raised in the country during the 1940's and 50's, we never locked the doors, even when we left and stayed gone all day. We didn't know where the keys were. These days, people will break into churches and steal. People steal from their businesses and even from their own families. God help us!

Prayer: Oh God, have mercy on us and give us hearts for honesty once again. In Jesus' Name, Amen.

MARCH 7

Telling the Truth

Exodus 20:16 "Thou shalt not bear false witness against thy neighbor."

It is easy to falsely accuse someone or make them look bad to make us look good or get something we want. The old folks believed that their word "should be their bond." Lying on a witness stand in a courtroom is a serious offense, because justice cannot be done on lies.

Gun trading used to be a favorite "sport." Too many times, someone would conceal a damaged one and try to deceive and get a better gun. That is lying.

Coons and squirrels are great "liars." They run up one tree and jump onto another one or "back track" to fool the dogs. Some people do that. If the pressure gets too great, if they have done something wrong, or if it will somehow enhance their position, people might lie.

Children and parents should practice telling the truth always. A family that lies to each other cannot build trust. Truth is one of the first building blocks to a good marriage, sound business dealings, and sound relationships.

Prayer: May every word I say come forth with compassion and truth. In Jesus' Name, Amen.

MARCH 8

Possessions in Perspective

Exodus 20:17 "Thou shalt not covet . . . anything that is thy neighbor's."

Someone gets a new gun, truck, deer stand, or something else, and pretty soon somebody else has one. At times, they can't afford it, and what they had was working fine. When we want something someone else has, that is coveting and sinful. Advertising is geared to cultivate it. Hunting magazines are full of ads that encourage us to covet and be dissatisfied with what we have. We become envious until we get a certain thing, and then it doesn't make us happy.

We have to learn that material possessions are not going to satisfy us. When you get them, you have more debt and are still unhappy. We need to change our minds and desire what really satisfies—a relationship to the Lord. He will be there in good times and bad. That new rifle or truck will get all scratched up. You get tired of every material thing, but He will never grow old. People get tired of their spouse and think they need a new one, but that doesn't work either. It is all selfishness. Focus on the Lord and others. You will be more at peace.

Prayer: Lord, help me to learn that more and better things never satisfy. Help me to get joy not out of things but serving You. In Jesus' Name, Amen.

MARCH 9

Protecting the Unborn

Exodus 21:22–23 "If men strive and hurt a woman with child, so that her fruit depart from her . . . and if mischief follow, then thou shalt give life for life."

We have referred briefly to this in another devotional, but it is worth more time. This passage says that if someone hurts a pregnant woman, she miscarries, and the baby dies, he shall be put to death. God values the unborn and counts them as human beings. The penalty for hurting one is stiff.

Man has a right to make laws to govern wildlife and preserve nature. We guard against hunters destroying eagles, spotted owls, and other creatures that are endangered with heavy fines or imprisonment.

Man is given the right and responsibility to protect human life as well. The death penalty was allowed by God for taking the life of the unborn. That is how precious they are to Him.

Prayer: Lord, the unborn are protected by You out of deep compassion. Let me be just as compassionate. In Jesus' Name, Amen.

MARCH 10

Responsibility

Exodus 22:5 "If a man shall put in his beast . . . and shall feed in another man's field . . . shall he make full restitution."

The Lord holds us responsible for our actions. Suppose a hunter is on a quail hunt with another person. The quail get up near the vehicle and he accidentally shoots a hole in the other hunter's truck. What is his obligation? I am not sure under state law, but morally he is obligated to repair the damage at his expense or that of his insurance company.

We make careless mistakes and sometimes resist making it right. In the Scripture lesson, the farmer allowed his beast to eat another man's field. God required that he restore the value lost. We are morally responsible for our own actions as well as those of our family and animals.

Prayer: Father, may I be willing to take responsibility—with a good attitude—for anything that violates others. In Jesus' Name, Amen.

MARCH 11

The Law of Love

Exodus 23:4 "If thou meet thine enemy's ox going astray, thou shalt surely bring it back to him again."

It is not uncommon to find someone's hunting dog walking beside the road in South Georgia. Sometimes they have their name collars on. The kind thing to do is catch the dog if you can, call the owner, and keep the dog for him until the hunter arrives. Otherwise, the hunter may never find him, or he could be killed in the road.

The main point here goes beyond just lost dogs. God's will is for us to keep our eyes open to ways we can help people without any desire for a reward or patting ourselves on the back. Don't suppose that someone stranded beside the road has a cell phone and help on the way. It is encouraging for someone just to stop anyway. When someone's house burns or they lose their job, don't presume that they have insurance or money stashed away. No law says we should do something, except the law of Christian love.

Our Scripture said even to do good to "our enemy." Jesus said, "Love your enemies," in Matthew 5:44, too. That is bigger than human nature and requires the Holy Spirit in our heart.

Prayer: Honestly, Lord, I would rather just avoid my enemies and save kindness for those who do the same to me, but I belong to You and You call me to higher living. I will obey. Amen.

MARCH 12

Gifted to Serve

Exodus 31:3 "I have filled him with the Spirit of God . . . in knowledge and in all manner of workmanship."

In this Bible verse, a man named Bezaleel was called upon by God to use his craftsmanship to build the house of the Lord.

Outdoorsmen have so many skills that we can use for God and man. We can just use them on ourselves or we can use them for others. Why not give some of our kill to nursing homes or the needy? With the bag limit on deer at a dozen now, there is no way we could use it all. Some of us are good carpenters, painters, or handymen. There are widows in our neighborhoods that could use some help. How about thinking of going somewhere with your church on a mission trip to build a church or work in Bible school? Miss a hunt or two. It may cost you some money, too. Sacrifice a little and give to others. If we look for ways, we can see how we can use our time, resources, and abilities for someone besides ourselves.

Prayer: Lord, I admit I am very selfish and lean toward only serving me and mine. Help me learn to look beyond myself. In Jesus' Name, Amen.

MARCH 13

Patience

Exodus 32:1 "When the people saw that Moses delayed to come down . . ."

Moses was on the mountain with God and the people became impatient with him and God and began to worship a golden calf. God would have destroyed them, but Moses prayed and He relented.

If you have ever hunted doves, you know that you have to be patient. You may get to the field at noon and not see one dove. I have been to some hunts where very few ever came in. Sometimes you wait two or three hours and very few come in. Some hunters get discouraged and leave. They miss all of the fun when the doves begin coming late in the day and you have your limit in a very few minutes.

We are very impatient these days. "Road rage" is a real problem. Some people have shot and killed other drivers simply because they got impatient with them on the highway. We get impatient with our spouse and children and even God because they don't do what we want done when we want it done. I used to get very angry when my dear wife didn't have supper by 6 PM. She, of course, had nothing else to do, since we had three small children. Ha! Impatience on our part indicates how self-centered we are and it does not please God. It shows we are bowing down to a worse god than a golden calf. It is ourselves!

The Bible says, "But they that wait upon the Lord shall renew their strength." (Isaiah 40:31)

Prayer: Lord, take away the selfish attitude I have at times that causes me to be impatient and become angry with others and You. In Your Name, Amen.

MARCH 14

A Learning Attitude

Exodus 32:9 "Behold, it is a stiff necked people."

Have you ever seen a "know it all" or one who is going to do it his way? People may suggest how or where to hunt or a gun to buy, and you do the opposite. Is your spouse or someone else encouraging you to go to church or read your Bible and you refuse? The Lord would call you "stiff necked." God hates pride and that is all it is. We don't have to do what everyone says, but when we are too proud to listen, we have a problem. Do we think we know all of the answers, and that no one has anything to offer us? When someone tells you something you really didn't know, do you lie by indicating that you did? If we would listen a little closer to people, we could learn from their wisdom. We would not appear to be so arrogant, either.

We complain about our children not wanting to learn in school, but we set a bad example by not continuing to learn ourselves. God wanted His people to listen and follow Him, and we should do that. We should read something other than sporting magazines and the sports page and broaden our minds. Pick up the Bible and read it. Find a good book about a Christian athlete and read it. Continue your education.

Prayer: Lord, first, help me to listen and obey You better, and then help me develop the precious mind you gave me. For Your glory, Amen.

MARCH 15

Knowing the Way

Exodus 33:13 "Show me now thy way, that I may know thee and find grace in thy sight."

This prayer of Moses shows his yearning to know and please God. Hunters of the right caliber read game regulations every year to make sure they know seasons, limits, and anything else in order to abide by the law. If they don't read, they won't know, and ignorance can put you in jail.

Most people would readily say, "I want to know God and benefit from His blessings." How many really try to get to know Him by reading the Bible, praying, and going to church? Do we do a better job preparing for hunting season than we do preparing to meet God? The game warden might give us a ticket for violations, but if we disobey God, we will regret it even worse. What a blessing it is to know God and sense His presence every day.

Prayer: Lord, help me know the way by getting my priorities straight and seeking You rather than just being a better hunter. In Jesus' Name, Amen.

MARCH 16

God's Care

Exodus 33:22 "I will put thee in the cleft of the rock, and will cover thee with my hand while I pass by."

Moses wanted to see the glory of God, and he could not, but God did pass by and overshadow him for protection.

Numerous episodes have been heard of hunters with more game in their possession than the limit, trembling as they watch helplessly while the game warden heads their way. Some run, but there is no where to go.

What about when the trials of life come and you are helpless and alone? That happens to all of us. We have had six untimely deaths in just our family. If you have not experienced it, you will. A word of hope is that God is always near. The finest Christians have trouble, but He will "cover you with His hand" and see you through if you trust in Him.

Prayer: Lord, sometimes we feel like we can't make it. Thank You that You are always there to cover us. Thank You, Amen.

MARCH 17

The Glow of God's Presence

Exodus 34:35 "And the children of Israel saw the face of Moses that the skin of Moses' face shone."

It is really not a secret when a hunter bags his limit, gets a big turkey, or a giant buck. There is a spring in his step and you can almost see him glowing. He tries to be under control, but he can't hide it.

When Moses went before the Lord and returned to the people, he had to put a veil on his face because it glowed. When I was a little boy, I had a little toy that, if you kept it in the light for a few minutes, it would glow in the dark. There is that same kind of glow about a committed Christian who has been in the presence of Jesus. He is at peace. All is right with the world, and his guilt and burdens are gone. It might not last if we fail to walk close to Him. It left Moses. The New Testament tells us that he continued to wear the veil to fool the people, but the glow was gone. Has the glow gone from your Christian life?

Prayer: Lord, the excitement of being a Christian is slipping away. Shine on me again so I can glow. In Jesus' Name, Amen.

MARCH 18

Generosity

Exodus 36:5 "The people (brought) more than enough for the service of the work."

When Israel was building the sanctuary, the people brought more than was needed to do it. Moses had to tell them not to bring any more materials.

Hunters and all other humans are either takers or givers. We can have an attitude of getting more for ourselves from nature and others, or giving back. I know people who are very generous in giving things from their company's business, but are very stingy with their own. Hunting club members are of two brands, either they wait on everyone else to carry the load, or they pitch in. We call the first ones "moochers." Some Christians go to church and give very little. They, too, are saying, "I'm keeping mine. You folks carry the load."

The Bible says, "It is more blessed to give than receive." (Acts 20:35) God is a giver. When people are not generous, they really think what they have is theirs, but it isn't. God owns it all. If you are generous, you are like Jesus.

Prayer: I have a tendency, Lord, to be stingy and keep things for myself. Make me generous like You. In Jesus' Name, Amen.

MARCH 19

Placing Blame

Exodus 32:24 "I cast it into the fire and there came out this calf."

I have been in a dove field shooting and hitting nothing and tried to blame everything under the sun—the birds, the color of the sky, the wind. I have even wondered if the shells had any shot in them. What I probably need is a little more practice!

Aaron had requested gold and jewelry from the people and had sculptured a calf for them to worship while Moses was with God on the holy mountain. When Moses returned and confronted him, Aaron claimed the calf just popped out of the fire on its own.

We try to remove guilt from ourselves by placing blame on parents, spouses, circumstances, and anything else we can these days. Parents and others may have set a bad example, but we, as adults, bear the blame for what we do. There are more temptations than there used to be, but we and we alone decide to resist or cave in.

There is no overwhelming force, including Satan, that compels us to be, say, or do something we have not agreed to do. We are not victims of fate. Until we take responsibility for our circumstances and make some changes, we are doomed to make the same bad decisions over and over again.

Prayer: Lord, I cannot blame family, society, or circumstances for my faults. Through Your power, help me to change. In Jesus' Name, Amen.

MARCH 20

Scapegoat

Leviticus 16:22 "And the goat shall bear upon him their iniquities unto a land not inhabited."

The goat described in the Scripture has been labeled the "scapegoat," because it symbolically took the sins of the people away. We use the term for someone who takes the blame for what others do.

We have hunted quail at times with two or more dogs. Every now and then you aren't seeing dogs, and then you hear quail flying. The immediate assumption is that "ole so and so" ran the birds up. You don't know for sure, because you didn't see it, but he got the blame. He is the "scapegoat."

The Bible says, Without the shedding of blood, there is no remission." (Hebrews 9:22) We need a "scapegoat," since our own blood won't suffice. Jesus agreed to come as God dressed like a man to shed His blood for us. If we believe in Him and obey, He will save us.

Prayer: Yes, Lord, I know I have sinned and need a "scapegoat." You are mine. Thank You, Amen.

MARCH 21

Acceptable Sex

Leviticus 18:20 "Thou shalt not lie carnally with thy neighbor's wife."

Regrettably, when some hunters gather at hunts, they glorify ungodly relationships, and sometimes pornography is present. If people want to see their marriages come apart in a hurry, they can participate in such. Christians just shouldn't be around that kind of thing. Only develop close relationships with those who are faithful to their spouse and who avoid inappropriate talk and behavior. Just quietly walk away.

The book of Leviticus dedicates almost an entire chapter outlining bad sexual relationships. Involvement with persons other than your spouse, such as other family members, animals, or another person of the same sex is condemned by God. That seems unnecessary to say. It is called "defilement" and was punishable by separation from the nation and death. The only acceptable relationship is between a man and his wife.

Prayer: Lord, keep me clean in my relationships, conversation, and thought. In Jesus' Name, Amen.

MARCH 22

Favoritism

Leviticus 19:15 "Thou shalt not respect the person of the poor, nor honor the person of the mighty."

I am told that wildlife will sometimes abandon their young because they are sick, injured, or defective in some way. They do so because they are animals and not made in the image of God.

It is easy to show favoritism because a person is wealthy or powerful and look down our nose at those who are not so fortunate. We can even be like animals and mistreat one of our own children by favoring one over the other.

We all have special friends and there is nothing wrong with that, but we should treat everyone with respect as creations of God, no matter what their status in life. If you put it in human perspective, the person you look down on and mistreat now, may be rich and powerful later.

Prayer: Dear Father, I have been shunned by people and it hurts. Help me treat everyone with respect. In Jesus' Name, Amen.

MARCH 23

Helping the Poor

Leviticus 23:22 "When ye reap the harvest of your land, thou shalt not make clean riddance of the corners."

There is a book in print now called *Looking Out for Number One* that was a bestseller. I haven't read it, but the title sends a message that is foreign to God. He teaches us to consider the poor. The verse told them to leave corners of the fields for poor people to have for food.

If you watch wild animals, you will see that they have no regard for other animals. Mothers do provide for their young, but when coyotes and various types of cats find food, they will run others off to keep them from eating. It is interesting to watch our hummingbird feeder. They are just plain mean. One will eat all he wants and then guard the feeder to keep others away.

There are people who could help themselves, and I try to encourage them to do so, but there are the handicapped and those who are temporarily out of work, as well as sick people, who really need help. God says that a person should help them.

Prayer: Lord, we have been so blessed. Give us the compassion to see a need and meet it. In Jesus' Name, Amen.

MARCH 24

God's Justice

Leviticus 26:23 "If ye . . . walk contrary unto me, then will I also walk contrary to you."

I had placed a ladder stand against a large tree and hunted it several times one season. After hunting season was over, we noticed that the tree had fallen. I could have been badly hurt if the timing had been different, because I had not noticed that the tree was rotting. It would have been my own fault. One day, I jumped out of my Ford Bronco and left it out of gear. It rolled down the hill and ran into the brick National Guard Armory and bent up the front of the truck.

Lean on a rotting tree, and you might get hurt. Leave loaded guns lying around, and it might cost someone their life. These principles are just common sense. By the same token, if we intentionally or ignorantly violate God's law, He holds us accountable. It might be here or hereafter. We cannot break God's law without it breaking us.

Prayer: I have a tendency, Lord, to do things that I know are wrong. Help me stop in my tracks before I self-destruct. In Jesus' Name, Amen.

MARCH 25

Jealousy

Numbers 5:14 "And the spirit of jealousy came upon him."

Very often, hunters are jealous when another one has a good hunt. It has been known to divide people and cause hard feelings. People can be jealous of their spouse as well. When the spouse pays too much attention to someone else, jealousy can arise, though it may not be justified. It is caused by lack of trust or insecurity. It is understandable these days with so much unfaithfulness. Sometimes a spouse is jealous of the time the mate spends hunting.

I agree that there is a big problem of neglect in some families when one works all week and then hunts every weekend from September to May. We must remember that our first responsibility, other than our relationship to God, is being a companion to our mate and parent to our children. We can't be that if we are never home. Sit down together as a family and agree on time to be spent together. A reasonable amount of time can be allocated for all.

Prayer: Jealousy is a problem for me sometimes, and it is unjustified. I turn that over to You and ask You to help me deal with it constructively, and help me allow adequate time for my family. Thank You, Father. Amen.

MARCH 26

Alcoholic Beverages

Numbers 6:3 "He shall separate himself from wine and strong drink . . ."

Drinking is dangerous when combined with guns. Even drinking in the evenings and hunting during the day is dangerous. The effects could endanger someone's life. Senses, reflexes, and judgment are dulled, and life is too precious to risk it.

The Bible verse is about taking a "Nazirite Vow." The person was setting himself aside for special service to the Lord, and it required sacrifice. A person who really wants to be all God wants him to be will make some sacrifices.

I think alcoholic beverages are never appropriate for a Christian. We set a bad example when we use them. I can influence some child to become an alcoholic. Alcoholism destroys families and leads often to poverty and ruin. We are warned about causing another person to stumble.

Prayer: Lord, I don't use alcohol myself, and I don't want to lead anyone astray. Deliver me from any desire for alcohol. For Your sake, Amen.

MARCH 27

Opposition

Numbers 12:1 "And Miriam and Aaron spoke against Moses."

I guess hunters can be the most negative people around at times. "Things are bad and getting worse," or "That will never work." Sometimes we oppose things and people for no apparent reason. Maybe it is resentment or jealousy. Honest disagreement is acceptable, but we should be supportive unless we have a solid reason not to be.

Moses' brother and sister, Aaron and Miriam, opposed him and found themselves opposing God. Moses went to the Lord with it. How do we respond to opposition? Rather than being mad and trying to defend ourselves, why not just accept it good naturedly and turn it over to the Lord? Jesus was accused and opposed on every side but did not answer a word. Be like Him.

Prayer: Lord, when people oppose me, I take it personally, get mad, and try to defend myself. Help me to rely on you to defend me. You are My Defender. Amen.

MARCH 28

The Anger of the Lord

Numbers 12:9–10 "The anger of the Lord was kindled against them and . . . Miriam became leprous."

Why did my deer stand fall and break my leg? Why is my marriage going sour? Why are my children not doing well in school? Everyone has bad things to happen to them. The Bible says that the rain "falls on the just and the unjust." (Matthew 5:45) However, the Bible also teaches that God can cause bad things to happen to us for disobedience. Jesus indicated that sometimes, not always, bad health is caused by it. The fact that your deer stand fell, your marriage is failing, and your children don't do well in school may be neglect of some sort.

When bad things do happen, though, the first place to look is our relationship to God and others. That is why Miriam got leprosy. God will let you know in your own heart if you are being punished for sin, and you won't have to guess. If you are being disciplined, make things right and go on. Next, look at your patterns of life. They may be causing problems—smoking, alcohol, people you hang out with, or other destructive behavior.

Prayer: Lord, make me more sensitive to You when I am having trouble, so I can avoid destroying myself and others. I'm listening. Amen.

MARCH 29

Confidence

Numbers 13:30 "We are well able to overcome it."

Some people go through life overcome by obstacles, and others are full of solutions. Hunters go into the woods saying why the hunt will be successful, and others complain that the moon isn't right, the wind is blowing wrong, and they left their grunt call at home.

Moses had sent twelve men to spy out Canaan so they could enter the land promised by God. Two came back with an attitude of confidence, but ten spoke of giants in the land. The two, Joshua and Caleb, saw the power of God, and the others saw the weakness of man.

Christians know that there will be obstacles and that things won't be just right, but God will be with them. They are positive and optimistic even in tough times. You might call it faith. Negativism discourages others and destroys confidence. Success is built on confidence. It encourages and helps others put their best foot forward so that they can tackle anything.

Prayer: Lord, You are my strength, and with You I can never fail. Thank You! Amen

MARCH 30

Consequences of Fear

Numbers 14:30 "Ye shall not come into the land."

The Israelites would not go into the land because of their fear of dangers, and they rebelled against God. The successful deer hunter fears nothing. They scout the deep woods with briars, water, mosquitoes, snakes and other dangers. They walk considerable distances under bad conditions until they find a good spot. A lesser approach will only yield fewer and inferior deer.

The fear of the Israelites was costly. That whole generation would die–except Joshua and Caleb, who were faithful—and not enter the Promised Land which flowed with plenty. Their fear was rebellion. We can also go our own way and rebel against God, but we pay for it with disappointment and a broken life.

Prayer: Lord, help me to operate by faith, not fear. I will trust You. Amen.

MARCH 31

Willful Disobedience

Numbers 15:29–30 "Ye shall have one law for him that sinneth through ignorance . . . but the soul that doeth ought presumptuously . . . reproacheth the Lord."

I was hunting doves one day and having a good shoot, so I wanted to make sure I stayed within the limit. I thought I counted twelve, so I stopped and left the field. When I was cleaning the birds, I found that I had thirteen. Fortunately I was not caught, because my error would likely not have made any difference to the game warden.

It does to God. There is a different law for those who innocently disobey than for those who do it willfully. That is a sign of a merciful God. Children have accidents, and their punishment should be less severe than if they intended to disobey.

Hebrews 10:26 says, "If we sin willfully after that we have received the knowledge of the truth, there remaineth no more sacrifice for sins." God expects us to avoid what is evil and do what we know is good, and He will judge accordingly.

Prayer: You are a merciful God. Help me never to intentionally disobey. In Jesus' Name, Amen.

APRIL 1

The Sin of Unbelief

Numbers 20:12 "Because ye believed me not, ye shall not bring this congregation into the land."

We may choose to reject hunting advice or what type of duck call to use and we may or may not miss out on game, but the stakes are much higher on whether or not to believe God. We may reject the Bible as God's Word, or even refuse to believe there is a God. Eternity is involved in those decisions, so don't make the wrong one.

Israel was in an uproar because they didn't have water. Moses and Aaron fell on their faces before the Lord, and He told them to speak to the rock and water would come out. They thought speaking was not enough, so they hit the rock two times. That made it appear that God didn't provide the water, but hitting the rock did. Because they did not believe, they missed God's blessings of going into Canaan.

Continuing to doubt God will cause us to be lost and we will miss heaven. That is no April fool!

Prayer: Lord, as one man prayed, "Lord, I believe. Help my unbelief." I will trust You. Amen.

APRIL 2

Promises to God

Numbers 30:2 "If a man vow a vow unto the Lord, He shall not break his word."

Do you and your hunting buddies keep your word? You might have a verbal agreement on things as simple as responsibilities in the camp, an elaborate hunting agreement, or an expensive gun trade and find that things can change fast in what you agreed upon. In the old days, a man's word was his bond. We were taught always to do what we promised. A contract on a business deal was not necessary. Today, if you don't have it in writing, you can't count on it.

If people cannot depend on us to follow through on what we have promised, we have no integrity. We call those "pie crust promises." They will break at any time. I want people to know that I am as good as my word.

God holds us accountable for what we promise. We might have gotten emotional and made promises to Him but failed to keep them. We had better ask Him to forgive us and keep our promises in the future.

Prayer: Forgive me for making promises I broke. Thank You, Amen.

APRIL 3

Time for Change

Deuteronomy 1:6 "Ye have dwelt long enough in this mount."

Quail hunting can't be done sitting beside a field and waiting like waiting for doves. It requires moving into the thick woods behind the dog and finding them wherever they went when they flew up. You have to cross water, briars, vines, and plowed fields. Only the stout-hearted go after them, but they are the successful hunters.

Israel had been at Mount Horeb for a long time and had not claimed the land that God had promised them. They had become a little lazy and complacent, dreading the hard work that lay ahead. Moses had to prod them on.

Spiritually, it is very easy to stagnate and quit growing. Also, a person might know something good that he should do but keeps putting it off. Have you "dwelt long enough in this mount?" Maybe it is time to take a step of faith. Get into His Word, spend time in prayer, and begin serving Him.

Prayer: Lord, help me never be satisfied with how close I am to You. Amen.

APRIL 4

The Great Commandment

Deuteronomy 6:5 "Thou shalt love the Lord thy God with all thine heart, and with all thy soul, and with all thy might."

Some people think all of the time about hunting. They watch the TV hunting shows, read the magazines, and talk about it all of the time. You can hardly get them to talk about anything else! They are either talking about the last hunt or planning for another one. When hunting season is over, they are miserable. That is their central focus of life. If others don't hunt, those who do not hunt are led to feel that since they don't hunt, they are second class.

That is a distorted life. Now there is nothing wrong with hunting per se, until it drowns out more important things, like God. Our verse makes it clear as to what our priorities should be. A wise man once said that our priorities should be God first, spouse and family second, job third, and other things below that. Once that gets out of balance, there is going to be a collision. Put God first.

Prayer: God, I have said I love You, but confess that I put You last at times. I now put You back in Your rightful place and will arrange my life accordingly. Help me. Amen.

APRIL 5

Selecting a Spouse

Deuteronomy 7:3 "Neither shalt thou make marriage with them."

I have never heard of foxes mixing with coyotes, quail mixing with doves, even whitetail deer mixing with mule deer. Some of this may happen, but it is unlikely.

The Bible commanded the Israelites not to marry the pagan people in Canaan, because it would turn them away from the Lord and then He would destroy them. As it turned out, they did intermarry later on. Even King Solomon did, and the Lord destroyed many of them and allowed some to be taken away to Babylon.

The New Testament says, "Do not be unequally yoked." That means that a Christian should never marry a non–Christian. Common faith, interests, culture, traditions, and values can help make a marriage work.

Prayer: Dear Father, help me to select a Christian spouse or to accept the one I already have as Your gift for life. In Him, Amen.

APRIL 6

Leadership

Deuteronomy 10:11 "Arise, take thy journey before the people."

In all of my days of deer hunting, I have always seen does leading the way as deer travel through the woods. The dominant buck is usually last. I believe the reason the Lord did it that way was to protect breeding stock.

For whatever the reason, people with leadership abilities emerge in life. God made Moses a leader and commanded him to step forth. Moses resisted with all his might, but God would not give such a critical task to just anyone, and He had been preparing Moses for it.

God chose the leader in every family to be the dad. To be the leader doesn't make him superior. What we need is kind, gentle, strong dads who teach the children, model a godly life, and discipline them when necessary. Statistics show that children are less likely to go astray when they have that kind of dad and a mother who spend time with them. They feel secure and loved, and that is the best environment.

Prayer: Lord, lead me and I will lead my family on Your path. I'm looking to You. Amen

APRIL 7

Led Astray

Deuteronomy 13:1–2 "If there arise among you a prophet or dreamer of dreams and he giveth you a sign or wonder . . . saying, let us go after other gods . . ."

Some men wanted to come to our place and hunt coons one night. I had not been in a certain section of the woods in many years, and we went there after dark. The dogs didn't find anything, and we trudged through vines, briars, and thick bushes for a couple of hours. We were tired and frustrated, because on that occasion, I was the wrong leader to follow.

Moses warned Israel about following the wrong teacher that would draw them away from God. That is a real danger for a person who doesn't know God's Word but is hungry. They are very vulnerable.

Make sure you learn the Bible from people you can trust. Check new ideas you hear thoroughly before you swallow them. If it does not teach that Jesus was God or born of a virgin, reject it altogether.

Prayer: Lord, I want to follow. Protect me from the wrong leaders. In Your Name, Amen.

APRIL 8

Innocent Blood

Deuteronomy 19:9–10 "Then shalt thou add three cities . . . that innocent blood be not shed in the land."

A hunter saw several deer coming through the woods and picked a nice buck. When he shot, the buck ran off, but a small doe standing beside him fell. Doe season was not in. Accidents do happen, but I am afraid the authorities would have met his story with a little doubt.

God, in His mercy, provided a law and cities for people who killed someone by accident. The person could go to one of the cities and stay without being pursued by people getting revenge. His story would be investigated, and he would get a fair trial.

Sometimes innocent people are accused, and their reputation is ruined before they know it. It is done through carelessness and even intentionally in order to destroy a person at times. A critical word is like a bullet that is fired and can't be recalled. The damage is done and may never be overcome. As God gives grace, we should try to shield the innocent from injustice and be careful what we say about others.

Prayer: May I never intentionally say things to damage others, and may I be on guard and discourage others who do the same. In Christ, Amen.

APRIL 9

A Rebellious Son

Deuteronomy 21:18–20 "If a man have a stubborn and rebellious son . . . all of the men of the city shall stone him with stones."

To train a really good hunter, you have to start early, then by the time he is of age, he knows gun safety, is a wise hunter, and is accurate with his shots. It is more enjoyable to be with him, he has more success, and it is safer, too.

That principle can be applied to raising children. Over and over we see sons or daughters committing terrible crimes, and parents have to see them pay the ultimate debt to society. How heartbreaking! Though the child made that decision and can blame no one else, some wise parenting early on probably could have prevented it.

It all starts by parents teaching children to be obedient. If you laugh at his rebellion when he is a toddler and don't take it seriously, you will cry later on. Psychologists say children have formed their character by the time they are six or seven, and it is hard for them to change later. They won't "grow out of it." It must be dealt with compassionately, patiently, and early.

Prayer: Lord, deliver me from rebellious children and give me wisdom to guide them early. In Jesus' Name, Amen.

APRIL 10

Good Stewardship

Deuteronomy 22:6–7 "If a bird's nest chance to be before thee . . . thou shalt let the dam go and take the young to thee."

My two brothers, James and Bill, and I were hunting quail one day and the dog pointed in some gall berry bushes. Bill saw them on the ground and shot. Not a bird flew! We were surprised and a little disappointed. All of the covey was gone. That was bad sportsmanship, anyway, but it was poor stewardship, too, since the covey could not reproduce.

God commanded conservation, and usually we were sensitive to that. God said that we shouldn't take the mother bird, but we could have the young ones to eat. Reproduction could go on, and He provided for more birds.

I believe that most hunters are careful conservationists. They put out food and minerals, abide by bag limits, and provide good habitat for animals. We should be sensitive to God's creation, because that's His will. It will be in our best interest as well.

Prayer: Lord, You have blessed us with such a beautiful world that brings us so much pleasure. Help us protect it for Your glory and our good. Thank You. Amen.

APRIL 11

The Protector

Deuteronomy 23:14 "For the Lord thy God walketh in the midst of the camp, to deliver thee, and to give up thine enemies."

I have never run across a bear while I have been hunting, but I understand there are some small black ones in the southern part of my home state of Georgia. When hunters get in trouble with them, it is usually because they get too close to their cubs. The mother will protect her cubs with her life.

Good parents know how to be wise protectors of their children. They protect them from physical, emotional, and spiritual harm but do not insulate them from due punishment. Teachers should be permitted to discipline in fair and just ways, even including spankings of younger children, without objection from parents.

God protects His children but does not insulate them from their foolish mistakes. Nothing happens to a child of God without Him allowing it for the child's own good.

Recently, I was using my nail gun to install some very old, hard boards. A nail shot into a board, bent, ricocheted off the nailing surface and the bent nail hit me in the temple. It didn't even break the skin! That was a hard head and God's protection.

Prayer: Thank You, Lord. You protect us without our knowing it more than we know. Thanks again, Amen.

APRIL 12

Divorce

Deuteronomy 24:1 "When a man hath taken a wife, and married her, and she find no favor in his eyes . . . then let him write a bill of divorcement."

This statement by Moses was given, according to Jesus, because of the "hardness of their hearts." Jesus gave only one acceptable reason for divorce—sex with another person.

When people marry, they will not know all of the partner's quirks and faults, like hunting too much or walking through the house with blood and mud on their feet. Love means accepting the person as they are and not expecting them to change. There should be times every now and then that a spouse may kindly point out a fault. This should be rare, by permission only, and for glaring reasons.

Criticism can destroy a relationship. Kindness, affirmation, and acceptance should dominate marriages, although sometimes it will be hard to do.

One wife was asked if she ever thought of divorce. She said, "Murder every now and then, but not divorce!" She is right about one thing. We should never even consider anything but working our problems out.

Prayer: Lord, Your Word says that you hate divorce. Help me to hate it just like You do. In Jesus' Name, Amen.

APRIL 13

Honest Business

Deuteronomy 25:15 "Thou shalt have a perfect and just weight."

I do a little wood refinishing, and a friend asked me to refinish the stock on a real antique "rabbit ears" double barrel shotgun in otherwise excellent condition. He was getting old, and I thought he would give me a chance to buy it. He even implied that he might give it to my son. When he died, we couldn't find it anywhere, and we figured out that he sold it. I felt that I had been deceived, since I didn't charge him for refinishing the gun.

In Old Testament days, evidently a merchant would have one scale for some and another if he wanted to jack up the price for someone else. God rejected that. He expects honest and straightforward business dealings.

My Grandmother Lord said that Pap, her husband and my grandpa, never made a trade but what he got "gypped." He was an honest person and would rather lose than cheat someone. My father-in-law, George McBride, was the same way. He built cabinets, and his prices we so low that he barely made a profit. He gave lots of work away. I believe these men knew what God said about "just weights."

Prayer: Help me to be honest in my dealings with everyone. In Jesus' Name, Amen.

APRIL 14

Remembering

Deuteronomy 27:2 "When ye shall pass over Jordan unto the land which the Lord giveth thee, thou shalt set up great stones."

There is a mount on my wall of a large buck I killed several years ago. I am very quick to show him off to anyone who will pay me any attention. We decorate him at Christmas and I even named him. He is still the biggest one I have ever killed, and I mounted him to remember the experience.

The stones mentioned in the Scripture were to serve as reminders to the children of Israel, for generations to come, of how God had blessed them. He had allowed them to escape their enslavement in Egypt and brought them safely to their new home.

Are you making good memories with your wife and children, speckled with notations of how God has blessed you? Sometimes we don't even think about it. Call attention to His blessings every now and then so that you and your family will remember, and God can get the credit.

Prayer: Lord, I soon forget how You have blessed us. I want to set up some "stones" so that I never forget. Thank You. Amen.

APRIL 15

Preparing for Old Age

Deuteronomy 31:2 "I am an hundred and twenty years old this day; I can no more go out and come in."

My son killed two nice ten point bucks over the past several years, but their tines were short and the flanks were thin. Also, their teeth indicated they were getting very old.

That happens to every living creature eventually. Body cells have a limited life and deteriorate over the years. Scientists might find a cure for cancer, heart disease, and other major killers, but eventually we all will die. I'm not being morbid, it is just the truth. We all know we need to avoid smoking, alcohol, and other drugs, as well as eat right, get plenty of fresh air, exercise, and rest to live longer. Even so, we need to prepare for getting old.

Prepare yourself mentally that your body and mind will continue to perform less efficiently. It is no disgrace, and we need to accept it. Someday you won't be able to keep up with the young hunters.

The Bible says that spiritually we can become "renewed day by day." (2 Corinthians 4:16) If we commit our lives to Christ, we can be prepared for death.

Prayer: Lord, it scared me to think about death until I began to trust You with it. Thank You that we don't have to fear old age. Amen.

APRIL 16

Forgetting God

Deuteronomy 32:15 "Then he forsook God which made him, and lightly esteemed the Rock of his salvation."

A person I know has hunted deer, elk, quail, and other kinds of wildlife in several countries and surprised me by saying, "I'm tired of deer hunting and would really rather see the young men kill one." He has been so dedicated so long to it that he has just burned out. I guess that is possible when you do it as much as he did.

The Bible story tells us that a man named Jeshuran got lazy and lax and forsook God. He worshipped other gods. God said, "I will hide my face from him." The Lord judged him and allowed the enemy to overtake him.

There is no problem with someone deciding he doesn't like hunting as much or quitting altogether, but watch out that you don't backslide spiritually. When you begin that, you'd better begin to pray and study the Word more.

Prayer: Lord, I often get a little lax in my faith. Pull me back to You. In Jesus' Name, Amen.

APRIL 17

Who Will Bury You?

Deuteronomy 34:6 "And He (the Lord) buried him (Moses) in a valley in the land of Moab."

After many years of hunting with me and pointing quail, ole Belle, my first bird dog, died. She was given to me by my father-in-law, and I raised her from a puppy. We buried her, and there were lots of tears.

Moses was probably honored more than any other man, because he was buried by God, Himself. He failed God at times, but he was called "the servant of God."

I have heard of children who had become so alienated from their parents that they didn't even go to their funeral. How sad! There is nothing sweeter, though, than to see the children and other family members tearfully gather around the bed holding hands and singing hymns as a parent goes to meet the Lord. Wouldn't it be great if all families loved each other that much?

Prayer: Lord, may I love so much that my spouse and children care when I die. In Jesus' Name, Amen.

APRIL 18

Keeping Your Word

Joshua 6:25 "And Joshua saved Rahab . . . because she hid the messengers."

When Joshua sent two men to spy out Jericho before they entered the city, Rahab, a woman in the city, helped them, and they promised to save her and her family when they camc to destroy the city. They kept their word, and she was allowed to live among the Israelites because of her good deed.

When we hunted squirrels with dogs, we depended on them to tell us when he had an animal up a tree and which tree it was. Sometimes we would get to the tree only to find nothing and were disappointed.

It is even more disappointing when people do not keep their word. Can people "bank on" what you say, or do they wonder whether you are a person of your word? God always does keep His Word.

Prayer: We know how bad it is to depend on someone and be disappointed. Help us keep our word like You do. In His Name, Amen.

APRIL 19

Influence of One

Joshua 7:13 "Thou canst not stand before thine enemies, until ye take away the accursed thing from among you."

Some hunters, one morning, had already slipped into the woods with their noiseless and odorless clothing on and quietly climbed into their deer stands. Another hunter came really late, making enough noise to raise the dead. You say, "Yeah, he messed up his hunt, didn't he?" Wrong! He messed up *everybody's* hunt.

Israel lost the first battle at Ai because of the disobedience of just one man. A man named Achan sinned, and they lost the battle because God was not with them. Achan confessed and was disciplined, and then they were able to take Ai.

One rotten apple can spoil the whole barrel. One person can give a church, team, family, or any other group a bad name. God does not hold us accountable for the sins of others, but people often do. A high profile person like a pastor, politician, or professional athlete can give their associates a bad name. We don't stand alone. What we do definitely affects others.

Prayer: Lord, I have heard, "what I do affects nobody but myself." How wrong we can be. Forgive us. Amen.

APRIL 20

The Counsel of the Lord

Joshua 9:14 "And the men . . . asked not the counsel at the mouth of the Lord."

Joshua was tricked and made a covenant with a nation he was ordered by God to destroy, and later he had to go to war to protect that enemy. The Scripture tells us he was deceived because he did not ask counsel of the Lord.

Some years ago, I got a permit and went hundreds of miles to hunt with a friend who told me he was new to that area, but we could hunt if I wanted to go. Needless to say, we found nothing. I can blame no one but myself. A guide could have given us good counsel, and we might have been successful.

The Scripture says, "In a multitude of counselors there is safety." (Proverbs 11:14) A person doesn't have to be very smart himself, if he will surround himself with wise, godly counselors. It is very unwise to make major decisions without much prayer, study of God's Word, and good advice from godly people. Don't let pride get in the way. Get advice.

Prayer: Lord, I have a tendency to make decisions without consulting You. I will seek You first from now on. Amen.

APRIL 21

Keep on Going

Joshua 14:12 "Now therefore give me this mountain."

Caleb was eighty-five years old and still looking for a challenge. He did not ask for fertile valleys but the mountains. His faith had been strong, and along with Joshua, he recommended that Israel go into Canaan forty years before they did. Joshua gave him the mountain he requested, and it was yet to be conquered, for the Canaanites still lived there.

Too many people are quitting too young and becoming inactive these days. I think it promotes bad health mentally, physically, emotionally, and even spiritually. People retire and watch TV, which is not good. My dad died at ninety-five and his mind was still as sharp as a briar. He could no longer hunt and was in a nursing home, but he stayed as active as possible.

Christians sometimes give up church work and no longer serve the Lord. They say they want to turn it over to the young people. What a waste! When you get old, stay active!

Prayer: Lord, never let me quit serving until You call me home. In Your Name, Amen.

APRIL 22

Holding Brothers Accountable

Joshua 22:16 "What trespass is this that ye have committed against the God of Israel, to turn away this day from following the Lord."

Some of the tribes of Israel who lived far from the house of God built an altar, and the other tribes were preparing to go to war with them for forsaking the Lord. Leaders of the tribes went to them for an explanation and a war was avoided, but the point was made. It is easy for us to compromise godly principles, so it is good for every Christian to have someone to hold him accountable. It should not be in a judgmental or harsh way, and it is not a matter of being a constant critic. There are times when a friend should privately raise a question about conduct and attitudes. It should go both ways, because we all fail.

Hunting groups are excellent environments to do this. Compromise is easier then. Everyone should feel free to help a brother when he is doing something dangerous, illegal, or immoral.

Prayer: Lord, help us to feel responsible for one another and not be offended when others call us to account. In Jesus' Name, Amen.

APRIL 23

Choosing in Advance

Joshua 24:15 "Chose you this day whom you will serve."

The hunting rules in our group require that we only take deer with at least eight points and well outside the ears, deformed or injured ones, and does in season. If we didn't establish rules in advance, we would be tempted to make them as we go, which would be disastrous to the herd.

Joshua challenged his people to choose that day whom they would serve. There would be times, Joshua knew, when they would be tempted, and this way, they would not have to choose when the pressure was on.

We have to do the same thing and make moral judgments in advance. As the old saying goes, "It is a bad time to be trying to decide whether you will be moral or not in the back seat of a car." Decisions to go to church every Sunday are not made each Sunday. Decisions to be faithful as a spouse are made in advance, not when temptations come. It is too late then.

Prayer: Lord, I decide to be a godly person and serve You beginning right now. Amen.

APRIL 24

Following the Lead

Joshua 24:31 "And Israel served the Lord all the days of Joshua."

I am told that the reason ducks and geese fly in formation is to conserve energy for the ones behind them on long flights. The lead bird parts the air and the ones behind position themselves so that there is less resistance. During the flight, the lead bird will drop back when he is tired and another will take his place.

Joshua was like that to Israel. He made godly decisions and set the right example, which made it easier. They forsook the Lord after he died.

It works that way today. People are looking for leaders. They are encouraged to live godly lives when others hold to their convictions, no matter what the price. Children follow what their parents and others do. People are watching us all of the time, and what we do and say gives permission for them to do the same thing.

Prayer: Lord, that is a heavy responsibility. May I be a good leader to follow. In Jesus' Name, Amen.

APRIL 25

No Guts, No Glory

Judges 4:9 "I will surely go with thee, notwithstanding the journey that thou takest shall not be for thine honor."

There comes a time when a person must stand alone. God called Barak to war against the enemies of Israel, but he would not go without Deborah, and the glory went to a woman rather than him.

When our children first began to hunt deer, they were hesitant to go by themselves to their stand in the dark, so I or a sibling went with them. That was fine, but there was a chance that the extra noise and scent would reduce their chances of success.

Often we face a decision of standing alone or going with others and sacrificing our convictions. Compromise causes guilt and reinforces bad behavior in others. Being accepted and pleasing everybody seems attractive but impossible, so you might as well do right and take your chances. It is lonely to stand alone and it takes guts, but rewards are worth it.

Prayer: Lord, give me the guts to stand alone. Amen

APRIL 26

Defeat by the Weak

Judges 4:21 "She went softly unto him, and smote the nail into his temples . . . for he was fast asleep and weary."

Have you ever learned how to trap quail? Make a wire basket with a hole on the bottom along the edge of one side. Place the hole on the ground and dig a hole in the ground under it leading to the outside. Place seed outside leading to the hole in the ground into the trap. The birds will have their heads down eating and go into the trap but never look down again to go back out the hole. It is a weakness that has cost many a quail his life. Don't do it, because it is illegal.

The Bible verse tells of a mighty warrior being killed by a woman without a struggle. He could have won any battle but was weak when he let down his guard.

So many times people live a faithful life and then destroy it in a weak moment. A wise man once said, "Never get too tired, hungry, lonely, or angry."

Prayer: Lord, protect me so that I will not fall. I will thank You. Amen.

APRIL 27

An Unlikely Hero

Judges 6:15 "Oh my Lord, wherewith shall I save Israel? . . . I am the least in my father's house."

A friend living in Atlanta decided he would ride out in the country during deer season with his rifle about ten o'clock one morning. He wasn't much of a hunter. As he was walking around, he heard a noise. Looking up a hill, he saw a big buck and shot him. I had been enduring bad weather hunting for years and had never killed one! His getting a big buck was highly unlikely to happen that late in the day.

Gideon was called by God to free Israel from their oppressors, but he came from a poor family with no status and was the most insignificant one of the bunch. He obeyed, and God used him in a mighty way.

Everyone has abilities and potential. All we need is motivation, patience, and hard work, and God will use us. Many have come from poor, uneducated, backward families and gone on to accomplish great things. Look at Abraham Lincoln. He was poor, unattractive, and lost several elections before he became president.

Prayer: How encouraging that You will give us the power to do what You have called us to do. Thank You. Amen.

APRIL 28

Power to Succeed

Judges 7:6 "And the number of them that lapped were . . . three hundred."

Early one cold morning as I hunted deer, I looked and a large deer was staring me in the eyes. I must have been asleep and snored or made some other noise. My weakness cost me a nice deer. God can use us in spite of our weaknesses for His purposes.

The Midianites were harassing Israel, and Gideon was called upon to deliver them. He was selecting his army and attracted thirty thousand, and God said that it was too many for Him to get the glory. Gideon went from that to three hundred fearless and cautious men and defeated Midian, which had a huge army.

God sometimes uses the weak to accomplish His work. Don't give up on yourself because of some weakness you might have. When He calls, just rely on His power. He doesn't need your ability, just your availability.

Prayer: Thank You that You can use even the least of us. In Your Name, Amen.

APRIL 29

Permissive Parents

Judges 14:3 "Is there never a woman . . . among all my people?"

Samson asked his parents to get him a wife from the Philistines, who were the enemy and worshipped other gods. They objected but did it anyway, and his new bride finally betrayed him and left him for another man. The ungodly things his parents did to try to please him turned out hurting him worse.

All wildlife that I know anything about tries to protect their young. I have heard that when a rattlesnake senses danger, she will swallow her young and spit them out again after the danger has passed. That might be uncomfortable for the little ones, but it preserves them in the long run.

Parents will have to deny children things to protect them. Teenagers want cars and get them too young and lose their lives. Parents let their children have too much freedom before they are able to handle it, and they wind up pregnant or on drugs. They allow children the freedom of not going to church, and that is spiritually deadly.

Prayer: Lord, give me conviction enough to deny my children some things that will endanger their souls. For Your sake, Amen.

APRIL 30

Choosing Friends

Judges 14:3 "Get her for me, for she pleaseth me well."

As a person enjoys the woods, he needs to learn what he can eat and what will harm him that grows wild. There are many berries that are delicious and nourishing. Others look good but are poisonous. Poke berries are beautiful but deadly. If you don't know the difference, you'd better find someone who does before you get lost and need something to eat.

Samson wanted to choose a wife based on beauty. Lots of people do that. There are some good-looking people out there who should be avoided. Someone said, "Beauty is only skin deep." That is true.

Don't be fooled by what a person looks like. Some will cover up their flaws, and you don't know it until it is too late. Get to know them and their family and friends. The way they treat their parents is how they will one day treat you. The old song is right, "Fools rush in."

Prayer: Lord, give me the patience and wisdom to select friends who are godly. In Your Name, Amen.

MAY 1

Bad Patterns

Judges 16:4 "He loved a woman . . . whose name was Delilah."

Hunters know that you find game because of their patterns. Wildlife, like humans, develops patterns. Wildlife will alter their patterns if there is a sign of danger, if food sources change, and because of other things. Humans need to determine what their destructive patterns are and adjust also. In Samson's case, it was pretty women. In just a small section of Scripture, he was duped by three of them, and the last cost him his sight and life.

People who keep getting into trouble aren't wise enough to change their patterns. Fast driving gets you tickets and might cause wrecks. Drugs and alcohol can kill you. Flirting with people other than your spouse will get you into trouble. Breaking hunting laws will catch up with you. Are you getting into the same messes all of the time? Change! Smart people see the mistakes of others and learn, others learn from their own mistakes, and unwise people continue to make the same mistakes over and over.

Prayer: Lord, help me see dangerous patterns in my life and change by Your power. In Jesus' Name, Amen.

MAY 2

The Wrong Crowd

Judges 16:30 "And Samson said, "Let me die with the Philistines."

We might say, "How sad. Samson had to die with the wrong crowd." That would seem to be true, but when you really look at it, he *was* the wrong crowd.

Hunters know that you can put a puppy with trained dogs and soon he will begin to hunt like they do. If they run rabbits, he will, too. If you want him to point quail only, keep him away from rabbit dogs.

Over the years, I have seen children "go bad." As I would help parents cope and reclaim the child, they often rationalize by saying, "He got in with the wrong crowd." That may be true in the beginning, but I have restrained myself from saying, "Yes, but now *he is the wrong crowd!*" It is always someone else's kids who are the wrong crowd. A first step toward recovering from anything is admitting that I have a problem—I am the wrong crowd. At that point, there is hope for taking steps to recovery.

Prayer: Lord, help me admit that I have faults and not blame it on "the wrong crowd." In Jesus' Name, Amen.

MAY 3

Right

Judges 21:25 "In those days there was no king in Israel and every man did what was right in his own eyes."

Suppose there was no law. At first glance, it sounds pretty good to me. There would be no game limits and no licenses to buy. There would be no closed hunting seasons and you could hunt anything at any time. There would be no speed limits. You could steal, kill, rape, or anything else without fear of punishment. The only problem is that other people could do those things to me and my family and that would be a chaotic time.

There must be laws. In other words, we must define what is right and wrong. Who should decide that, humans or a higher, more intelligent Power? Proverbs 14:12 says, "There is a way which seemeth right unto a man, but the end thereof are the ways of death."

Almighty God has decided what is right and wrong, and it is recorded in the Bible, His Word. If it is not obeyed, civilization will cease to exist.

Prayer: Lord, thank You for laws and boundaries that maintain order and tell us what is right. Amen.

MAY 4

Loyalty

Ruth 1:16 "Thy people shall be my people and thy God my God."

A little boy wandered away from his home in rural North Carolina one cold day. His family and others looked day and night for several days and finally found the little fellow, but he had frozen to death. The interesting thing was that his old dog was still with him snuggled close by his side.

In the Bible story, Naomi's two sons had died and left their wives with their mother. She tried to convince them to go back to their parents and Orpah did, but Ruth made the beautiful statement above that is often used in weddings. She would stay and help Naomi earn a living. She later married Boaz and had a son who would be a forefather of the Lord Jesus.

Loyalty to family and friends is an honorable quality, as is loyalty to our country. The Bible says, "A man that hath friends must show himself friendly." (Proverbs 18:24) The same is true for loyalty. Loyalty to others will often make them loyal to you.

Prayer: Help me to be loyal to others, but most of all, let me be loyal to You. In Jesus' Name, Amen.

MAY 5

Giving Children to the Lord

1 Samuel 1:27–28 "For this child I prayed . . . I have lent him to the Lord."

Often men want to have a son to be a buddy while they hunt and enjoy the out of doors together. The man may have a son, but usually, the son would rather be with boys his own age. It was a selfish wish, in the first place. Rather than wanting the son to belong to God, he wanted him for himself.

Hannah had no children and prayed for years to have one. You would think she would keep him close to home, spoil him rotten, and then grieve herself to death when he grew up and left home. Some men and women do that. Surprisingly, Hannah weaned him and took him, as a toddler, a long way from home to the Prophet Eli to be raised in the house of the Lord.

Hannah is a good model for us today. We might not send them away as toddlers, but we should be training them from birth and praying that God would use them. When a child feels called to foreign missions, parents sometimes discourage it, rather than being humbled that God would bless them like that.

Prayer: Dear Lord, I release my children and grandchildren to You to be used and do Your will in whatever way You ask. They are Yours. Amen.

MAY 6

The Silence of God

1 Samuel 3:1 "The word of the Lord was precious in those days; there was no open vision."

With all of the clamor of traffic in the air and on the ground these days, it is a very special moment when it is very still, dark, and silent before daylight in a deer stand or duck blind. You can hear a sparrow walking through the dry leaves. What a peaceful time for the soul to rest and to talk to God.

It would be a frightening thing if you thought God was not speaking, yet the Bible reports a time like that when "there was no open vision." That is not God's doing, but man's.

If you are not hearing God, these are some reasons. You are not His child, you are not close to Him, you are not listening, or you have sin that you have not confessed to God and forsaken.

Prayer: Lord, I want to hear You, so I will confess and forsake any sin You reveal to me. Draw me nearer to you. In Jesus' Name, Amen.

MAY 7

Knowing the Lord

1 Samuel 3:7 "Samuel did not yet know the Lord."

Turkey calling is really an art. You may know all of the yelps, clucks, etc., but if you do the wrong thing at the wrong time, or too much, or not enough, you might never see a gobbler for Thanksgiving dinner. They will know you are a fake or not think you are one of them.

Samuel was a young boy and did not yet know the voice of the Lord. The Lord spoke, and Samuel thought it was the Prophet Eli. This happened three times before he was able to understand God's message. God was speaking, but he did not understand.

We can know *about* the Lord, as Samuel did, but not know *Him.* James 2:19 says, "Devils believe and tremble." Devils believe there is a God and fear Him, but have no relationship with Him. We know Him if we hear, believe, and become more and more like Him.

Prayer: I want to know You, not just believe You exist. Give me faith to know You. In Your Name, Amen.

MAY 8

Hungry for God

1 Samuel 3:19 "(Samuel) did let none of His (God's) words fall to the ground."

My son and I were walking in our yard one day near planted pines and he said, "Listen!" I stopped and listened but did not hear anything. He heard the squeaking of little mice that were being stalked by a king snake. I would have missed it, because I could not hear it. In other words, I let it "fall to the ground."

Samuel did not let God's Word fall on deaf ears. He hung on every word and applied them to his life, came to know God, and became a prophet.

We hear lots of preaching, read the Bible, and see godly people every day. It too often falls on deaf ears. We miss the meaning, and it makes no difference to our lives. If we were hungry for God, that would never happen.

Prayer: Lord, make me sensitive to Your Word, that I may change to be like You. In Jesus' Name, Amen.

MAY 9

Established

1 Samuel 3:20 "And Israel knew . . . that Samuel was established to be a prophet of the Lord."

Millard Warren, my wife's uncle, became a field representative of one of the major ammunition and gun manufacturers. Why do you suppose that happened? Many things entered into it, I am sure. He was a hunter all of his life, a crack shot with many types of guns, and outgoing in his personality with good salesmanship skills. It didn't happen by accident.

Samuel was not in position to be a prophet by birth. The sons of Eli would have the advantage there, but they were rejected by God because of sin. Samuel just proved himself worthy of the task by being faithful.

Some people "pull strings," "play politics," and otherwise try to push their way to the top, as I have in the past. Faith causes people to work hard, be patient, deal fairly with others, and wait on the Lord. God is in charge of our success. We don't have to force it.

Prayer: Lord, I am ready to do whatever You will through me for Your glory. You work it out. I will just be faithful and prepare myself. In Jesus' Name, Amen.

MAY 10

A Nation Rejects God

1 Samuel 8:5 "Make us a king to judge us like all the nations."

Selecting guides is something I rarely do, because those kinds of hunts are very expensive. If I was selecting one, I would make sure of his integrity, track record, and that he knew where the game was. I have known of hunters who hired guides who turned out to be phonies.

Israel had a choice of either having the reign of God through his prophets or having a dictatorship. They chose the dictatorship because surrounding nations had them, and also some of the prophets they had were corrupt. Samuel was discouraged by the decision. God told him that the people had not rejected him, but God.

Many people are critical of churches, pastors, Christians, and anything else that might have anything to do with religion. One famous pastor recently said that a person who does that has moral problems in his life that he is trying to justify. I agree. Jesus came to establish His church and when we refuse to be a part, we reject Him. Are you rejecting God?

Prayer: I want You to rule over me. Let me never be guilty of criticizing anything of which You approve. In Jesus' Name, Amen.

MAY 11

Timing is Everything

1 Samuel 11:15 "All the people went to Gilgal and there they made Saul King."

Dove hunting is a difficult sport, and only a few people are really good at it. If the truth was known, most people make less than twenty-five percent of their shots. As a dove passes, you have to lead him just right based on his speed, the distance, the type of gun shells, and other variables. It's all about timing.

Saul was wise in his timing about when to exert himself as king. He had been chosen by Samuel several years before, but just continued what he was doing until an opportunity came to show himself capable in battle. Then he was well accepted. That took patience.

Ecclesiastes tells us that there is a time for everything. Timely words can be consoling. At other times, the same words might be inappropriate. Constructive criticism can be good if done in the right way at the right time. Let God's Spirit guide you. He will give you peace about what to say or do and when to do it. The Bible also says that words well spoken are like "apples of gold." (Proverbs 25:11)

Prayer: Let me be so close to You that I know what to say and do and when to do it. I will wait on You. Amen.

MAY 12

Letting Children Mature

1 Samuel 17:28 "With whom hath thou left those few sheep?"

Deer, turkeys and other wildlife grow up and mature and seem to assume their role of adulthood well. A dominant buck and tom turkeys will attempt to prevent upcoming males from assuming their role, but in time, they do.

Eliab, David's oldest brother, was criticizing and trying to discourage David from confronting Goliath the giant to prevent a war. Maybe Eliab was a little ashamed that he was too afraid to take Goliath on. Shepherding sheep could be done by a boy or even girls, but the giant was different.

Brothers sometimes try to keep the dominant role they always had in the family as children. Parents do that to their children, also, and resist allowing them to be responsible adults. Mothers, particularly, want to continue to be mothers, and dads still want to control their kids. Children have to gradually be freed and allowed to fail. They need to know that parents and older siblings have confidence in them to function as adults.

Prayer: Help me to mature, Lord, and to encourage my children and siblings do the same. In Jesus' Name, Amen.

MAY 13

Right Confidence

1 Samuel 17:37 "The Lord delivered me . . . (and) he will deliver me out of the hand of the Philistine."

When a young person is introduced to the woods for the first time, he might be a little tentative. I remember being doubtful that I could hit a deer when I shot. Over the years, with experience, I became more confident in my abilities to operate in the woods and feel very much at home there.

David was trying to convince King Saul that he had the experience and skill to confront Goliath. Saul seemed to be convinced when David told him he was trusting in God. God did intervene and David dispatched the giant.

Our real confidence in life should not be in ourselves, but God. We are so limited, and God is so powerful. When we are young, we feel like we don't need God. There will be times in all of our lives when He literally has to carry us. The more we trust God and see His faithfulness, the more confidence we have in Him and the more peace we have. It is a stretch at first, but like a muscle, the more we exercise it, the stronger it gets.

Prayer: Lord, thank You that I can do all things through Christ who strengthens me. In Your Name, Amen.

MAY 14

Power in Behavior

1 Samuel 18:14–15 "David behaved himself wisely . . . and he (Saul) was afraid of him."

David earned a great deal of respect from Saul just by conduct and evidence that God was with him. Actually, Saul feared him because he saw him as a threat.

As I sat in my tree stand one morning, suddenly a flock of turkeys began making all kinds of noise and came running across the hill with their heads down. I don't know what spooked them, but it probably was a bobcat, coyote or fox. They didn't stay around, because they had probably seen one like him catch and eat one of their relatives before.

Now we don't want people to fear us in that same sense, but if you want the respect of people around you, just act in respectable ways. Dependability, honesty, and other Christian attitudes and values are respected even by non-believers. You don't have to say much.

Prayer: Lord, help me to act in such a way that people will see You in me. Amen.

MAY 15

Accepting Blame

1 Samuel 25:24 "Upon me, my lord, upon me let this iniquity be."

In this verse, Abigail is accepting blame for her husband, Nabal, who had refused to accommodate David and his men. This is a rare quality for people to accept blame for their own mistakes and even more so to accept blame for someone else. She was trying to keep David from killing him, in spite of his foolishness and insensitivity. David had protected them, and Nabal did not show any gratitude.

What do you do when you are hunting and accidentally shoot something that is illegal? Say you have called up a gobbler and you accidentally kill the hen that is with him, or you are shooting ducks and you mistake a pintail for a mallard? Most people would hide the game or try to sneak them out without getting caught. What if the game warden catches you?

People are very hesitant to take blame for their own faults. Admitting you are guilty or made a mistake is very hard, but it is important in the life of us all. We don't want to do it because it makes us look bad, but it really makes people respect us more. I've had to admit I was wrong many times to my wife and even my children. It takes a load off my mind. We aren't perfect and shouldn't even pretend we are.

Prayer: Lord, I want to be open and honest. Help me to accept blame and admit wrong. In Jesus, Name, Amen.

MAY 16

End Justify the Means?

1 Samuel 26:11 "The Lord forbid that I should stretch forth my hand against the Lord's anointed."

King Saul had been searching for David to kill him, and David could have turned the tables while Saul slept. Abishai, one of David's men, volunteered to do it for him, but David refused. Nobody would have blamed David, but he was "a man after God's own heart." (1 Samuel 13:14)

Bending the rules a little bit or stretching the truth is a great temptation at times while involved in hunting. We think it won't make any difference, or that it might actually make things better in the long run. We can want our way immediately and so badly that we make some bad mistakes.

I've known people that stole things from where they worked because they felt that they were underpaid. Grocery store clerks walk by the bananas and eat one without paying for it. Recently, in a grocery store, I noticed that most of the sealed bags of grapes had been torn open. Abusing company time is popular today. Many show up late for work, leave early, or abuse break times. None of this was as big as David's decision not to kill Saul, but it is still dishonest. We can't justify it as Christians.

Prayer: Lord, I know that if I break Your law, it cannot be justified for any reason. Help me to be godly at all times. In Jesus' Name, Amen.

MAY 17

Suicide is Not the Answer

1 Samuel 31:4 "Saul took a sword and fell upon it."

The senses of wildlife are keen for a purpose. Their ears hear better than humans', doves can see a grain of corn on the ground from fifty feet up, and deer can smell things from unbelievable distances that people can't smell up close. It is all for the purpose of staying alive. Some people jokingly say that possums are so ugly that they commit suicide, and that is why there are so many that are victims of "road kill." Of course, it isn't true. Animals are trying to survive, while so many humans are committing suicide.

How sad to see even young people doing that. Saul took his life to avoid the torture of the enemy and an agonizing death. The battle had gone sour, and he was wounded. He asked his armor bearer to kill him, but he had too much respect for human life.

We have no right to take our own life under any circumstances. It is cowardly, because we don't want to face reality. It leaves a family filled with guilt, regret, and unbearable suffering. It dumps your problems on someone else. It also encourages others to do the same thing. Never think of suicide, but if you do, talk to somebody fast. Talk to God and lay all your burdens on Him. See a pastor or Christian counselor.

Prayer: Lord, help me to remember that I can never get so low that You can't solve my problems. Help me to never take the easy way out, and to instead put my faith in You. In Jesus' Name, Amen.

MAY 18

Taking False Credit

2 Samuel 1:10 "So I stood upon him, and slew him."

A young man was reporting to David about how Saul had died by claiming that he did it to gain favor of David. We already know that Saul killed himself. It backfired on the young man, because David had him dispatched for killing Saul. The young man lied to claim credit and it cost him his life.

Hunters have been known to buy elk, deer or other mounts—even reproductions of trophy mounts—and claim them as their own kill. It is an ego thing, but a person who does it must feel very empty inside.

So many times bosses do not give credit to a worker who deserves it, but take the credit themselves. It destroys respect for them and kills motivation. I have had that happen to me at times.

Just do a superior job and be patient. You don't have to take false credit. People will notice and you will succeed.

Prayer: Lord, help me to be honest about my successes and failures and watch You give me glory in Your time. In Jesus' Name, Amen.

MAY 19

Praise for Enemies

2 Samuel 1:23 "Saul and Jonathan were lovely and pleasant in their lives."

It is hard even for family to brag on another hunter for a good shot, big kill, excellent dog, pretty gun, or actually for anything. When a compliment should be made, we usually swallow hard, become jealous, and say nothing. We miss an opportunity to build someone up.

David had been pursued by Saul for years. Since Saul tried to kill David, you would think he would have gloated when Saul died. David knew he would become king, and his enemy was gone. David actually lamented his death and called on Israel to weep. That takes a big man.

The secular world is learning that people hate for you to criticize and ridicule even your worst enemy. Politicians are learning that negative politics can hurt you. Coaches compliment teams that beat them or lose to them. A gracious, godly person is big enough to speak kindly of their competition. Husbands and wives should be free in their honest praise of each other and their children.

Prayer: Lord, help me be ready to speak words of praise to anyone, friend or foe, who has succeeded. In Jesus' Name, Amen.

MAY 20

Making Things Right

2 Samuel 2:26 "Shall the sword devour forever?"

Joab was in hot pursuit of Abner for killing his brother during a war. Abner was trying to call a truce and avoid further bloodshed. Joab agreed, and the civil war between Judah and Israel ended.

Two close friends who were in Sunday School together, hunted together, and vacationed together had a disagreement over a dog. Now they never speak to each other, and the friendship is apparently over. Both of them, down inside, are being eaten up by resentment, and it also affects their relationship to God.

Solving something like that takes something people don't naturally have—humility. Pride is the opposite, and we all have lots of that. Jesus said that if we go to the altar and remember someone has something against us, we shouldn't give our offering because it won't be accepted. Go to the person and make it right.

Prayer: Lord, at times I am full of grudges, ill will and wrong relationships that separate me from others and from You. Give me the humility to make things right. In Jesus' Name, Amen.

MAY 21

Revenge

2 Samuel 3:27 "Joab took him (Abner) aside . . . and smote him, therefore, for the blood of Asahel his brother."

What appeared to be a truce was not. Joab had been waiting for the right moment and killed Abner. This caused trouble that spread to David and his kingdom.

Many times, rather than making things right, we gossip to others and create more problems and ill will. Sometimes we try to "get them back" by doing something bad to them, something they own, or someone they love. It divides families, friends, churches, and marriages. How much better it would be if the two people involved could just sit down and make peace.

Revenge is taking matters into our own hands and making others "pay" for what they did to us. When we seek revenge, we take things out of God's hands. "Vengeance belongeth unto me, I will recompense," saith the Lord. (Hebrews 10:30) Stop the matter in its tracks. Forgive and try to forget about it. God will make it right, and you won't mess up your good name.

Prayer: Lord, I turn it over to You. Help me to forgive and forget. Amen.

MAY 22

Anger with the Lord

2 Samuel 6:7–8 "The anger of the Lord was kindled against Uzzah and God smote him for his error . . . and David was displeased."

A man and his son were hunting in the mountains before the days of hunter orange. They became separated, and the son was hunting down in a valley below the man. Seeing the bushes move and observing some brown, the man shot and killed his son. When things like that happen, people sometimes say, "Where was God?" Well, God didn't cause it to happen. As hard as it sounds, the dad must take the blame. He had a hard time dealing with it, I am sure, but time and the comfort of God and others will bring peace in due time.

Too often, blaming God becomes anger toward Him, as it did with David. It shifts the burden of guilt, maybe, but drives a wedge between people and God. They leave the church and become bitter toward ministers and the whole world. Others are drawn closer to God and use tragedy to bring glory to Him.

Remember, God loves us and can take bad things and work them for good. Accept His love. Cry out to Him and He will give you peace.

Prayer: Dear Lord, search me for anger that I might have toward You. I confess and forsake it. Amen.

MAY 23

Jealousy of the Spiritual

2 Samuel 6:16 "Michal . . . saw King David leaping and dancing before the Lord; and she despised him in her heart."

David's wife, Michal, resented David's conduct, as indicated in our verse, when the ark of the Lord was recovered and returned to Jerusalem. Apparently, he stripped naked before other women as he danced before the Lord and celebrated. His behavior was repulsive, but his desire to worship was commendable.

As we look around ourselves and see others serving the Lord, worshiping, and talking about spiritual things, we sometimes become resentful. We call them "holy Joes," fanatics, or some other unkind thing. Could that be jealousy or our wishing that we were that close to God? Different people are comfortable with different styles of worship, and as long as they don't disobey the Bible, we should not worry about it.

Rather than judging them or being jealous, why don't we encourage them and draw closer to God ourselves?

Prayer: Dear Lord, may I be encouraging to those who worship You, even if their style might be a little different. In Jesus' Name, Amen.

MAY 24

Humility

2 Samuel 7:18 "Who am I, Lord God and what is my house, that thou hast brought me hitherto?"

Why is it that one hunter gets the trophy bucks and others close by see nothing but does and spikes? For some, there are valid reasons. They make too much noise getting to the stand and squirm once they're in the stand. Finding places where there are big buck tracks is another, but there is another reason as well, and David "hit the nail on the head." God plays a role.

"Who am I . . . that thou hast brought me hitherto?" He recognized that God plays a hand in everything, and for some reason, God had made him king. He didn't deserve it and was humbling himself before God.

I am not saying that the better Christian you are the bigger deer you will kill and the more quail you will find. When things do happen in our favor, we need to remember where it came from. That is humility and thankfulness.

Prayer: Lord, thank You for who You are and the good things that You bring our way. Every good and perfect gift comes from You. Amen.

MAY 25

Kindness Gone Sour

2 Samuel 10:2–3 "Then said David, "I will show kindness to Hanun . . ." "Hath not David rather sent his servants unto thee, to search the city and to spy?"

David wanted to comfort Hanun when Nahash, his father, who had helped David, died. Hanun's men convinced him that David's men were not coming to comfort him, but were spies. Hanun humiliated David's men rather than receive their kindness, resulting in a bloody war.

Rugged outdoorsmen don't usually think about showing kindness like David, but we should. We think it is weak, but it is Christ-like to be kind and considerate. When we do this, we should not be surprised for people to be skeptical and say, "What does he want?"

It really doesn't matter how our kindness is received. We are looking to God for approval, not man.

Prayer: Lord, help us to be less concerned about what others think and just be like You. In Your Name, Amen.

MAY 26

Avoiding Lust

2 Samuel 11:2 "And from the roof, he saw a woman washing herself, and the woman was very beautiful to look upon."

When you are in a duck blind and have your bag limit, it is hard to leave when they are still coming in and you have plenty of shells. You just have to discipline yourself and leave, or you may find yourself in serious trouble.

David was idle and letting his eyes wander. Rather than turning his head and going in another direction, he noticed the woman's beauty, and wound up pursuing and seducing her, then having her husband killed to cover it up. It destroyed his family and the Kingdom of Israel.

All of us are capable of that. We have to nip it in the bud. It is far easier to look the other way than get involved, ruin your reputation, and destroy your family. These days, many men and some women read pornographic magazines and visit such websites, which just cultivate lust. Stop it! You do not satisfy your sexual appetite by reading such trash, gawking at women, or having an affair. You make it worse. The only answer is to stop encouraging such thinking. The alternative is heartache and damage you can never overcome.

Prayer: Lust is such a powerful force, Lord, and is used by Satan to destroy so many families. Help me avoid it "like the plague." In Jesus' Name, Amen.

MAY 27

David's Crisis

2 Samuel 11:5 "And the woman conceived and sent and told David, and said, I am with child."

David's compromise caught up with him. Bathsheba was pregnant, and her husband, Uriah, was away at war. Israel stoned immoral women, and she hoped the king could help her avoid that. Rather than facing the facts and doing what was right, David sent to the battlefield for Uriah. David hoped he would come home and spend the night with his wife so it would appear to be his baby.

Early one opening day of deer season, I was driving down the interstate when a small buck in the median panicked and ran out in front of me. Being hit at seventy miles an hour, there wasn't much left of him or the front end of my new Tundra. If he had stayed where he was, I would not have spent eight thousand dollars to repair my truck, but he made that fatal mistake.

When you find yourself in a crisis or have made a mistake, don't dig in deeper by telling lies or making other mistakes to cover it up. Face up to it, take your lumps, and make things right. The sooner you do it, the easier it will be.

Prayer: Lord, help me face my problems head on and make things right. In Jesus' Name, Amen.

MAY 28

Uriah's Big Heart

2 Samuel 11:13 "(Uriah) went out to lie on his bed with the servants of his lord, but went not down to his house."

David's plot failed because of Uriah's loyalty to his fellow warriors. He would not enjoy the comforts of home and family while his comrades were sleeping in the field and eating "army chow."

That is refreshing in light of the "every man for himself" mentality we sometimes see. I have observed so many times, that a parent takes a son or daughter hunting and puts them in the very best location—where the parent usually hunts—or that a son cleans the deer for his parent.

Jesus said, "Greater love hath no man than this, that a man lay down his life for his friends." (John 15:13) I think of so many men and women in our country who have sacrificed their convenience, and sometimes their lives, that we may be free. God bless them all!

Prayer: Lord, thank you for unselfish people, big-hearted people, who think of others rather than themselves. They bless us. In Jesus' Name, Amen.

MAY 29

David's Darker Side

2 Samuel 11:15 "Set ye Uriah in the forefront of the hottest battle and retire ye from him, that he may be smitten and die."

The next step in David's evil plot was to get Uriah killed so he could marry Uriah's wife in order to cover up the immorality that left her pregnant with David's child. He continued to pile evil upon evil to protect himself.

I am reminded of how settlers moved into the West in the 1800's slaughtering herds of buffalo for their hides and leaving the livelihood of the Indians to rot in the sun. They did not care if great numbers of Indians starved. David showed the same kind of calloused thinking.

No one is above what David did. I shudder to think where I would be or what evil I might have done if Christ had not saved me and I had not been influenced by godly people.

Prayer: Lord, deliver me from that frightening darker side and my tendency toward evil. In Jesus' Name, Amen.

MAY 30

Smoothing Things Over

2 Samuel 11:25 "Let not this thing displease you, for the sword devoureth one as well as the other."

David had commanded Joab to put Uriah in danger and allow him to be killed. The reason he sent this message to Joab was to cover his own guilt. Surely Joab lost a great deal of respect for David that would never be regained.

This is nothing compared to what David did, but even intentionally violating wildlife laws or the way we treat our bird dog can stick in someone's mind and damage our Christian witness. Bending the rules and telling "white lies" sends a powerful message to children that can't be "smoothed over."

We need to be very careful what we do and say. What we do can be damaging to the thinking others have about God and Christians, since we claim to be Christians. We are accountable for it when we turn people away from the faith. Jesus said, "But whoso shall offend one of these little ones which believe in me it were better for him that a millstone were hanged around his neck and that he were drowned in the depth of the sea." (Matthew 18:6)

Prayer: Lord, help me never to do anything that I have to later smooth over or cover up. In Jesus' Name, Amen.

MAY 31

The Truth Comes Out

2 Samuel 12:7 "Thou art the man."

Nathan the prophet came to David and confronted him about what he had done. He told a story of a rich man who had guests and slaughtered the only pet lamb a poor man had and fed them. David became angry and said anyone who did such a thing should be killed. Nathan said, "You are the man!"

David immediately confessed and repented. Nathan said the Lord had forgiven him, but the Lord would, "raise evil against thee out of thine own house." It happened that Absalom, David's son, led a coup attempt and tried to kill David and take his wives.

A game warden tells of a man who had been hunting deer illegally for years. The warden vowed to catch him and waited all hours of the day and night, and he finally caught him. Sometimes it takes a long time, but truth finally comes out and justice is done, because the all-seeing eye of God never sleeps. We cannot hide from God. Justice will be done either in this life or heaven.

Prayer: Lord, since we cannot hide from You and justice will be done, help us to live pure lives. In Jesus' Name, Amen.

JUNE 1

Torn Apart

Psalm 32:3 "When I kept silent, my bones waxed old."

One afternoon as I was sitting in my deer stand, a big black coyote came walking out of the woods toward me. They have become a real problem in our area, and we shoot every one we see. It was a long shot and I did not make a clean kill, so the animal yelped and whined. I was finally able to get the scope on him again and put him away. I felt really bad seeing him suffer like that. "Guilty" is the right word. I don't think it was wrong, but it tore me up inside. David's failure was planned, and he had reason to feel far worse than I did.

Psalm 32 is about David's reaction after he was confronted about his sin with Bathsheba. It is hard to say why there was such a lapse that allowed him to stoop so low. It began to eat him up. Godly people feel that way when they do wrong. Some hardened criminals have no conscience, I am told, but Christians do. When there is no repentance, some doctors would say that the anxiety could cause ulcers or even cancer of the stomach. Depression could result. I am convinced that guilt can destroy you mentally, emotionally, physically, and spiritually for sure. It tore David apart.

So many people are filled with guilt over things they consider to be small, but no unforgiven sin is small.

Prayer: Lord, bring to my mind anything that I have done wrong and not made right. I will confess and forsake it. Amen.

JUNE 2

Forgiven

Psalm 32:5 "I said, I will confess my transgressions unto the Lord; and Thou forgavest the iniquity of my sin."

David could have denied what he had done and tried to continue to cover it up. He could not cover it up from God or the people either. There could be no peace until he confessed it to God. He did, and God forgave him. Verse 1 of this chapter says, "Blessed is the one whose transgression is forgiven."

It is a feeling of freedom to be forgiven. To know you can look yourself and others in the eye is priceless. You don't have to hang your head in shame anymore.

I mentioned in an earlier devotion about the guilt of shooting thirty-eight doves and how I felt after breaking the law. Setting the bad example before the other hunters really bothered me. When I apologized to them, they seemed to think I was strange, but I felt clean again. What a great feeling it is to know you are forgiven and that you are right with God and others!

Prayer: Thank You that You died on the cross so that we wouldn't have to bear our guilt. In Your Name, Amen.

JUNE 3

Fruit of Failure

2 Samuel 13:14 "Being stronger than she, forced her and lay with her."

The fruit of David's failure, though God forgave him, produced the same in his children. A son, Amnon, raped a daughter, Tamar, and Absalom, another son, retaliated by killing Amnon. Absalom attempted later to kill David and did temporarily drive him from the throne, and he even raped David's wives. The sin of David was the beginning of the end and wound up destroying his family and dividing Israel.

Pesticides and land management, over a period of years, has damaged the quail population. We may recover with the new management practices, but I'm not sure. Sin is like that. Though we can be forgiven by God, it impacts us forever.

We might say that taking a drink or doing this or that won't hurt, but it does. Our children and others watch us closely and sometimes exaggerate what we do. The drink you take, or some other thing they see you doing, might not affect one child, but it could influence another to do the same thing to an extreme and later on destroy his family. What a terrible price to pay for committing some "small" sin.

Prayer: Lord, reduce the impact of my failures on my children and change me to be a better influence. In Jesus' Name, Amen.

JUNE 4

Breeding Discontent

2 Samuel 15:2 "When any man that had a controversy came to the king for judgment, Absalom called to him."

David's son, Absalom, was destroying the credibility of his dad by indicating to them that David either was unable or unwilling to solve their problems. The son soon won the hearts of the people so that they rebelled against David and started a war.

The Bible lists breeding discontent as one of the six things God hates—"he that soweth discord among brethren." (Proverbs 6:19) A loose tongue can destroy the reputation of a good man by making condemning inferences that cast doubt on his character. I've seen it done on the job and around the hunting camp.

It might be something like, "I believe this person might be hunting on your land." This could create ill will with no evidence to support it. It might also be "Well, I don't know if you can trust him or not." It is sinful to make derogatory statements about people whether they are true or not, unless it is strictly to someone who can help.

Prayer: Lord, You have said, "Blessed are the peacemakers," so help me not to breed discontent. In Jesus' Name, Amen.

JUNE 5

The Providence of God

2 Samuel 17:7 "Hushai said to Absalom, the counsel that Ahitophel hath given is not good a this time."

It was Absalom's plan to kill David, his dad, and become king, and he asked advice of the two men mentioned. Ahitophel actually gave the best advice for that purpose, but God led Absalom to listen to Hushai to accomplish His purpose. David could not be destroyed at that time, because God was on his side and still had something for him to do.

Homing pigeons are interesting birds to me. When we lived in Atlanta, a friend would take some into South Carolina and release them. They would circle a time or two and then go on their way. Though he would drive straight back home without stopping, they would beat him back. The friend said that because of radar and other interferences some would get lost and wind up in downtown Atlanta. Most of them, though, had the ability to find their way home, by some means unknown to man.

God never gets confused and is working His will. Since He knows where He is taking us and we don't, doesn't it make sense for us to stay close to Him? He is leading us home.

Prayer: Lord, Your plan is perfect and You are making it happen. Help me to follow You home. In Jesus' Name, Amen.

JUNE 6

Humble Leadership

2 Samuel 18:4 "And the king said unto them, what seemeth you best, I will do."

Many times as I have hunted quail with my dog, I would say, "Why is she sniffing around over there? The birds are more likely to be over here." More often than not, she was right.

King David wanted to go with his people to war. Idleness had gotten him into trouble years before. The people loved the king, and he was getting old so they didn't want to risk his life. They asked him not to go, and he agreed to the will of the people.

Leaders need to lead, but there are times when they need to listen to the advice of others. Good leaders surround themselves with competent people and not "yes men." If a person has the "my way or the highway" mentality and is hard-headed, the people won't follow him for long. Couples need to listen to one another as well and be willing to consider another opinion. In some families, one dominates all of the time. A "know it all" is filled with pride and soon loses his following.

Prayer: Lord, let me be humble enough to listen to advice. In Jesus' Name, Amen.

JUNE 7

Losses

2 Samuel 18:33 "O my son Absalom! Would God I had died for thee . . ."

Though Absalom had betrayed, defamed, and tried to kill his dad, David, the pain for David was heavy. Absalom had been killed by Joab's young men in the war while he was hanging from a tree by his hair. David was grieving so hard that he could not celebrate the victory of his army, which discouraged them.

We have lost two adult sons-in-law at very early ages and a baby granddaughter, so we can understand David's loss, at least to some degree. A friend of my wife lost a son serving as a military pilot and they still grieve after a year.

If you know someone with such a loss, spend time with him. Take him hunting. Encourage him to read Psalms in the Bible and spend lots of time in prayer. If you have lost someone special, talk about it with friends and family and go to church. You may need to see a Christian counselor if you can't seem to move on with your life. May God bless you and give you strength.

Prayer: Lord, we know You carry us when we can't carry ourselves. We depend on You. Thank You. Amen.

JUNE 8

Feeling Secure

2 Samuel 24:2 "Go now through all the tribes . . . and number ye the people."

King David had a very large kingdom and had handily defeated all of his enemies with God's help. We are not sure why he wanted to count the people. Joab, his general, saw no need for it. It could have been so David would feel more secure. God objected, probably because of that reason, which indicated that David lacked faith. David should have been looking to Him, not warriors.

We had an old bird dog that was terribly afraid of bad weather. When the thunder began to roll, she went under whatever she could find close by and shook like a leaf. That is understandable. Lots of people, as well, are afraid of bad weather.

What is our ultimate source of security—our money, our guns, the government, or some person? If we rely on them, we can be sure there will be a time when they will not be enough. If we put our trust in God, then there is no time when we should be afraid.

Prayer: The Bible (Psalm 23:4) says, "Though I walk through the valley of the shadow of death, I will fear no evil." Thank You for that comforting promise. Amen.

JUNE 9

Sacrifice

2 Samuel 24:24 "I will not offer burnt offerings unto the Lord my God of that which dost cost me nothing."

God had commanded David to build an altar on the property of a man named Araunah. The man wanted to donate the property rather than sell it. David insisted on buying it so that it would be a true offering to the Lord.

The story is told of the chicken and hog discussing breakfast for the landlord. The chicken suggested to the hog, "I'll provide the eggs if you will provide the bacon." The hog refused saying, "Yours would be an offering, mine would be a sacrifice."

David was on target, a commitment to the Lord calls for sacrificing time, talent, and money. We have to realize that what we have belongs to Him, not us.

Prayer: Lord, all we have really belongs to You. Help us be willing to offer it freely. In Jesus' Name, Amen.

JUNE 10

Holding Children Accountable

1 Kings 1:6 "His father had not displeased him at any time in saying, why hast thou done so."

Adonijah, another one of David's sons, rebelled and wanted to become king in David's old age. Scripture says it was because David didn't hold him accountable when he was a boy.

Hunters who train coon dogs will not tolerate them treeing anything but a coon. If the person goes to a tree and finds a possum, bobcat, or anything but a coon, or if the dog runs off chasing deer, the dog is severely disciplined. Soon, a good dog will not pay attention to anything else but a coon.

Having raised three of our own, Martha and I have learned that it is painful for parents and children to hold them accountable. It is far easier to turn a deaf ear and hope they will grow out of their disobedience. Old folks used to say that you can get crooks out of an oak when it is a sprout, but it is almost impossible when it gets older. It is true about children. They set their life pattern very early.

Prayer: Lord, help us to bend little minds and wills early, so that law enforcement won't have to break them later. In Jesus' Name, Amen.

JUNE 11

Changes in Leadership

1 Kings 1:43 "Our lord King David hath made Solomon king."

Shifts in leadership are painful for some and welcomed by others. As the dominant buck gets older, sooner or later a younger, stronger one comes on the scene and takes over. That is the way it has to be for deer to survive. It is usually with a life and death struggle.

David was coming to the end of his reign, and Adonijah had declared himself king. Solomon was David's choice. Adonijah and his leaders were killed, and the rest scattered. It was a violent thing.

It is good to live in a country where changes in government are without bloodshed. Companies change management. You might have had a supervisory change and thought you should have gotten the job.

When leadership changes and you are displeased, the best way is to have an attitude of cooperation and do the best you can to do a quality job. Be patient and trust God to work things out.

Prayer: Lord, change is hard. I will do my best and trust in You. In Jesus' Name, Amen.

JUNE 12

Tooting Your Own Horn

1 Kings 1:5 "Adonijah, the son of Haggith exalted himself, saying I will be king."

Bucks paw scrapes in the ground and rub on trees with their antlers during the "rut" to attract the attention of prospective does. That is good for him, but it also tips hunters off about his location and could cost him his life.

Adonijah wasn't asked, or elected to be king, he chose himself. As we will see later, he attracted quite a bit of attention that did cost him his life.

How does a person get that promotion? Some people try and even succeed by "tooting their own horn" or pushing their way in. The best way is to serve. In the long run, it is how people perform and their attitude that wins out. The old saying, "toot your own horn because nobody else will" usually fails and turns people off.

Prayer: Lord, You know what You want me to do and be. I will be faithful, work hard, and let You toot my horn. Amen.

JUNE 13

Source of Wisdom

1 Kings 3:9 "Give thy servant an understanding heart to judge thy people."

Many years ago, a family member offered me a bird dog puppy and let me have the "pick of the litter." I didn't know how to choose the best dog based on markings of an eight week old puppy. As they were being fed, I noticed one that, rather than scrapping with the others, took something and went off by herself to eat. I didn't know what that meant, whether good instinct or independence, but she impressed me and I chose her. She made a good dog, as many of the others did, so the choice was good.

Solomon had been made king of Israel and God told him, "Ask what I shall give thee." Solomon didn't ask for personal things like wealth, so God granted his wish for "an understanding heart," and he was regarded as the wisest man who ever lived.

True wisdom to handle our business, raise our family, and live our lives comes only from God. When we agree to love Him and follow His will, He will give us the wisdom we need to be obedient.

Prayer: Lord, I will obey You. Give me the wisdom I need to follow. In Jesus' Name, Amen.

JUNE 14

God's Wisdom

1 Kings 3:28 "They saw that the wisdom of God was in him to do judgment."

These days, if you are fortunate enough to find a covey of wild quail, you only get covey shooting. They go into the thickest woods and close places where it is hard to shoot fast enough. Only hunters who are "quick on the draw" get birds. We wouldn't call that wisdom, but it surely is good instinct.

Solomon had to decide between two prostitutes who claimed the same baby. He said, "Cut it in two and give half to each." One of them agreed and the other said, "Give her the living child and don't slay it." Solomon gave that woman the child, and Israel respected the judgment of the king from then on.

How do people know when to trust your judgment? They see you make godly decisions. The more you do it, the more they value your advice. By the same token, when people see you make impulsive, unwise choices, they won't listen to you. People know when you are giving them godly wisdom. It is scriptural and it just rings true.

Prayer: Lord, if I am to be used by You, I must act and speak wisely. Give me wisdom. In Jesus' Name, Amen.

JUNE 15

An Unwise Choice

1 Kings 11:4 "His wives turned his heart after other gods."

Solomon took seven hundred wives and three hundred concubines, in many cases to assure good business relationships with neighboring countries, and he became very wealthy because of it. As a part of accommodating them, he would be obligated to worship their gods. He forsook God.

Many young people have been raised in the church and have gone off to college, only to be led astray by ungodly teaching and other things that appear to be attractive. They fight the battle between their early faith and a desire to be accepted, which is their new god. Some return when they have children of their own, others never do.

Solomon would later write, "all is vanity" in Ecclesiastes, because he shelved his commitment to God. He became very depressed in his old age. An unwise choice can be overcome by asking God's forgiveness and turning back.

Prayer: Lord, I have neglected You over and over. I am weak. Help me overcome it. In Jesus' Name, Amen.

JUNE 16

Listening to Counsel

1 Kings 12:13 "And the king answered the people roughly and forsook the old men's counsel."

Rehoboam had become king after Solomon and alienated the people so that Israel and Judah separated and went to war. He had threatened heavier burdens, taking the advice of his young friends rather than a little softer approach from the older men.

In making the major decisions of life, some make them based on opinions of the ones they normally hang around with. That is a good way to get the answer you want rather than the answer you need. Younger people might be more idealistic and not want to hear from older people who are more realistic. Get advice from both and then make a wise decision after much prayer.

A young man was given a tip from his aging dad about some hunting and investment land at a great price. He accepted that advice and made a good choice. The dad also recommended a surveyor who was eighty years old and the young man made the mistake of taking that advice, too. Because of the thick woods, the old surveyor only cut off seventy-five acres rather than the one hundred acres the young man could have bought. Good sound judgment on the part of the young man would have avoided that.

Prayer: Lord, help me weigh advice from many sources and pray to You for the best decision. In Jesus' Name, Amen.

JUNE 17

Conflicting Voices

1 Kings 13:18 "I am a prophet as thou art; and an angel spake to me by the words of the Lord."

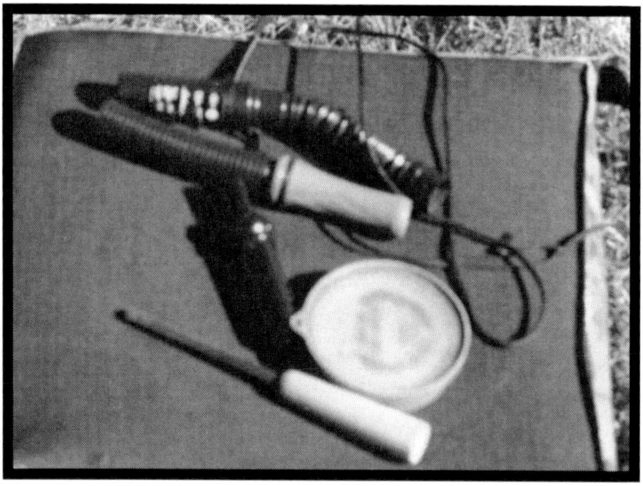

A prophet of God was warned not to go to a certain place, and another prophet came with another word "from the Lord" that conflicted with it. The first prophet "bit the bait" and went. He was killed because he listened to another man rather than God.

Hunters use all sorts of calls to deceive animals and get them in range. I have a "grunt call" for deer that is supposed to bleat like a fawn, grunt like a doe, or grunt like a buck, young or old. However, I have only been sure that a deer responded once. Some people say they have better luck with calls.

There are many voices out there, but we generally know which one is right. If you hear from God, don't be talked out of it. Good and godly people will try to change your mind because of their own interests. Remember, if God wants you to do something, He will tell you directly. If you know it was God, go for it! You won't regret it.

Prayer: Help me to know Your voice and follow. In Your Name, Amen.

JUNE 18

Disguise

1 Kings 14:5 "She shall feign herself to be another woman."

Hunters are masters of disguise. We disguise ourselves to be an oak, pine, or even snow. We do a good job fooling ducks, deer, and turkeys. The amount of game we get is evidence of good disguise. By the way, we still got lots of game before all of these new hunting clothes came out, and we did it by hiding behind trees and bushes or sticking limbs in our hats and button holes. We had nothing but our own scent and noises we could make with our mouth or a stick. It would really be sporting today if we still did that, but now I am in trouble with the merchandisers.

A woman with a sick son disguised herself from the prophet of God in order to get a favorable opinion on whether her son would live or die. God informed the prophet so that when the woman arrived, the old blind prophet heard her feet and called her by name.

We can fool animals and even other people with the "false fronts" we put up, but we can't fool God. His all-seeing eye knows even our thoughts.

Prayer: Lord, help me be pure so I won't have to try to hide things from You or other people. Thank You. Amen.

JUNE 19

Making a Decision

1 Kings 18:21 "How long halt ye between two opinions?"

Many years ago, I was trying to "enjoy" too many different hobbies. I was flying planes, golfing, hunting, and fishing. That left little time for a family of a wife and three children, so I dropped my two most expensive—flying and golf. That was a good decision.

Elijah the prophet was telling Israel that they had to decide between other gods and God. After a dramatic display of God's power, they decided to follow God for a while.

Life is full of decisions. We have to get the best information and best advice possible and decide. Some people have a hard time doing that and delay until they have to make a quick decision, which is likely to be a bad one.

People delay trusting the Lord with their lives, because they think it will restrict them in some way or take all the fun out of life. They wait too late, until their life is ruined. If we don't decide "for" we decide "against." Why wait? Chose faith in Christ now.

Prayer: Lord, I've waited long enough and am taking a big risk. I surrender now. For Jesus' sake, Amen.

JUNE 20

Standing Alone

1 Kings 19:10 "I, even I, only am left."

Elijah had destroyed the false prophets Israel worshipped, but a woman named Jezebel swore to kill him. Now Elijah was on the run, exhausted, hungry, and depressed. As he talked about it to the angel, he complained of being the only servant of God left. The angel told him of hundreds of people that were serving God.

Hunting by myself isn't one of my favorite things to do. It is a lot more fun to have my children with me. It is safer, too, to have someone else along, but I will go by myself every now and then.

It is also hard to stand alone when the whole world, seemingly, is compromising. The drinking, off-color jokes, sexually explicit language, or even using God's name in vain are rampant. Dishonesty, lying, and immorality are everywhere. It seems that people have no clue what it is to serve the Lord. When you don't take part, you stick out like a sore thumb. We need to remember that when we find ourselves standing alone, that is when we can make the biggest difference!

Prayer: Lord, sometimes serving You faithfully is lonely. I need to be reminded that others are being faithful, and You are with us. Thank You. Amen.

JUNE 21

Training Our Replacement

1 Kings 19:19 "Elijah passed him and cast his mantle upon him."

For a few years until the quail population got so low, I tried to keep a trained bird dog. You can buy trained ones for a high price or raise your own. We would keep a female, breed her, raise a puppy, and train it. That worked pretty well.

Elijah was getting old, so God commanded him to anoint Elisha to take his place. He did so simply by throwing his coat on him. Elisha followed him around for a while until Elijah was taken up into heaven by a whirlwind.

We all are getting older and should be training someone to take our place in our business, church work, or wherever we are involved. We should spend lots of time training our children about life. Above all, we should be teaching people about the Lord. If everyone trained two, we would have twice as many to tell others about Jesus after we are gone.

Prayer: Lord, I won't last forever, and the work must go on. Help me to plant my life in someone else. In Jesus' Name, Amen.

JUNE 22

Faithful Student

2 Kings 2:2 "As the soul liveth . . . I will not leave thee."

Hunters today have access to a tremendous amount of information about hunting. There are magazines, books, videos, etc., on the finer points of hunting almost everything legal. For example, you can learn every sound that a turkey makes and under what conditions they make it, and buy calls that sound like them. People buy them like mad because they want to be successful.

Elijah was called of God to go to Jericho and wanted to leave his student, Elisha, behind. Elisha would not stay, I think, because he wanted to learn all he could from the old prophet about serving the Lord.

People who are not Christians should search for enough information to make an intelligent decision about whether or not to follow Christ and not reject Him out of ignorance. Christians can grow by being hungry to learn through Sunday School, personal Bible reading, and worship. If it is important to learn how to call turkeys, surely it is even more important to know the Lord.

Prayer: Lord, create a hunger in me to be a faithful student of Jesus. In His Name, Amen.

JUNE 23

A Double Portion

2 Kings 2:9 "I pray thee, let a double portion of thy spirit be upon me."

Several years ago, I received an autographed cap of one of the famous inventors of camouflage patterns for hunting clothes. He is on videos and TV programs having successful hunts and admired by many. I suppose many young hunters are saying, "Man, I wish I was like him."

Elijah was about to leave for heaven and asked Elisha what he wanted to be given to him. His answer was to give him a double portion of his spirit. Just what he meant is not certain. Was it enthusiasm, charisma, a close walk with God, or maybe his attitude? Maybe all of the above is the answer.

I ask people to pray for me that I have a combination of what Solomon and Elisha asked, namely, God's wisdom and a double portion of His spirit. Wouldn't it be great to have the wisdom of God and a gracious spirit to use it?

Prayer: Lord, I am struck by this like Elisha. Give me Your spirit of love, understanding, and compassion. In Jesus' Name, Amen.

JUNE 24

Picking up the Mantel

2 Kings 2:14 "(Elisha) took the mantel of Elijah that fell from him."

My great grandfather Green assumed the role of provider for great-great grandma and five children in 1861, when his three older brothers left for the Civil War. Great-great grandpa had been dead for several years. At fifteen years of age, great grandpa took on a big job, but they made it.

Elijah was gone and his coat lay on the ground as a symbol of the unfinished work of the Lord. Elisha could have left it there and gone back to his farming. Instead, he followed through and blessed God's people for many years.

Non-productivity is a problem in the business world today. I have been there and noticed a great deal of lost time because of hunting. People are talking and thinking about it when they should be "picking up the coat" of the company's work. Another thing that is even more important is the Lord's work that we neglect for sports.

We can enjoy hunting and refresh ourselves, but let's not leave the mantel on the ground.

Prayer: Lord, may I never shirk my responsibility to my family, church, and job to entertain myself. In Jesus' Name, Amen.

JUNE 25

God Through Music

2 Kings 3:15 "When the minstrel played, the hand of the Lord came upon him."

I have heard of people using recordings to hunt animals. Predators can be attracted by hearing recordings of prey in distress. Crows can be called in by sounds of crows. I think using recordings is legal in some states for some types of wildlife.

Elisha was seeking the will of God for the king of Judah and some foreign kings who had come to him. He asked them to call musicians and God spoke to him while the musicians were playing. He was able to give the Word of the Lord to the kings.

There are many types of music out there, much of which has words that are damaging. They talk of murder, sex, and many other things that promote evil things and dishonor God. There are many songs that are inspirational and encourage good things, teach God's Word, and help us love the Lord more. Listen to music that makes you worship. Set some of your radio buttons to Christian radio stations.

Prayer: Thank You for gifted people who bring us beautiful music that honors You and builds us up. May I only listen to music that does that. In Jesus' Name, Amen.

JUNE 26

God Blesses Kindness

2 Kings 4:16 "About this season . . . thou shalt embrace a son."

A woman and her husband saw Elisha passing by their home often and decided to build a place for him to rest. Elisha wanted to do something for them, but the woman gave no suggestion. Elisha's servant noticed that they were very old and had no children. Elisha promised the woman a son and God granted one. That was the desire of her very heart.

My father-in-law, was a kind and generous man that loved to hunt. He never owned land to hunt on, but as he served the farmers in his work, and otherwise, they often volunteered to let him hunt on their land. Because of his unselfish, Christian way, they were glad to let him.

I am convinced that God gives faithful people the desires of their heart. Psalm 37:4 reads, "Delight thyself also in the Lord, and He will give you the desires of your heart." They don't even have to ask, because they might not even realize what their real desire is.

Prayer: Lord, You have given me things I wanted deep down so many times that I didn't realize I could have. Thank You. Amen.

JUNE 27

Blessings God's Way

2 Kings 5:10 "Go and wash in Jordan seven times . . . and thou shalt be clean."

When my brothers and I were boys, a thing called "itch" plagued just about every family, and medicines for it were not available. We smeared our bodies with "tallow" (dried cow fat), and sulfur and wore the same long johns for about a week. We stunk to high heaven and felt very dirty, but I guess it worked. The itch went away.

A Syrian general called Naaman was a leper and looked for cures for that disabling and deadly disease. He learned about Elisha being able to talk to God and maybe heal him. Upon hearing from the general, Elisha sent his servant to tell Naaman to dip seven times in the dirty Jordan River in Israel. Naaman was furious, saying the rivers in Syria were just as good. He finally did as Elisha said and was healed.

God may answer the prayers of obedient people and give something different, but it will always be better. When we pray, we should look for answers but be open to unusual ways that we don't expect. Then give Him the praise.

Prayer: Lord, I will pray, but give me what You want to and when You want me to have it. You will give me Your best for my good. I trust You, Amen.

JUNE 28

The Spirit World

2 Kings 6:17 "The Lord opened eyes of the young man and, behold, the mountain was full of horses and chariots of fire round about Elisha."

Have you ever been deer hunting in your tree stand, constantly and carefully easing your head around to see, and without hearing a sound, a deer appears, standing right in front of you? It makes you wonder if they can't become invisible and visible at will. I have had it happen to me and it is kind of spooky.

Elisha had been telling Israel's king every move Syria made, and Israel had escaped them several times. Wondering why, Syria's king was told that Elisha knew what was going on in his bedroom. Therefore he sent a mighty army to capture Elisha. Elisha's servant saw the army and became afraid until God opened his spiritual eyes and he was able to see the army of God protecting them.

There are unseen beings everywhere, according to the Bible. It speaks of angels (Gabriel, Michael) in large numbers. Jesus said that He could have called many angels to defend Him at the crucifixion. The devil has angels and God does, too. Both are fighting to control our lives and we decide who will win by the decisions we make. Christians have the Holy Spirit in us and if we yield to Him, He will guide us.

Prayer: I yield myself to Your control, Lord. Protect me and use me for good. Thank You. Amen.

JUNE 29

Half Way Commitment

2 Kings 14:3–4 "He did according to all things his father did, howbeit, the high places were not taken away."

This is the epitaph of Amaziah, a king of Israel. He served God in many ways but fell short by not tearing down the "high places," or altars the people used for worshiping other gods. This is a sign that his heart did not totally belong to the Lord.

When I first began to hunt, I was in my stand early in the morning no matter how cold or windy or rainy it might be. I have been there when it was fifteen degrees or when it was so warm that mosquitoes would buzz all around me. I have changed over the years. It seems as though I look for excuses to stay in bed.

If we are not careful, our dedication to the Lord can be like that. We can do like Amaziah and say, "I'm doing pretty well. Nobody is perfect, and some of these little things I do aren't hurting anybody but myself." That is what makes unhappy Christians. We claim to be His but won't give ourselves to Him completely. Those "high places" become temptations to backslide.

Prayer: Lord, I give up those things I know you aren't pleased with. I don't want to be a "half way" Christian. Help me. In Jesus' Name, Amen.

JUNE 30

Gradual Deterioration

2 Kings 17:6 "The king of Assyria carried Israel away into Assyria."

Coyotes have become a big problem in our part of the country. They have, I think, accelerated the gradual depletion of the population of quail and other wildlife. Packs of them have no problem destroying farmers' calves. They are threats to goat and sheep herds. They started in our section, I am told, when fox hunters began to import them as fox population decreased. Coyote numbers then increased to where they are today.

Israel had strayed further and further away from God. He had been patient and raised up judges to rescue them, but finally, He allowed Assyria to take over.

Sin is like that. We slip here and there and neglect worship, prayer, and service. Before we know it, we are not acting like a child of God at all. Chastisement comes next, where our loving God allows calamity to draw us back to Him.

Prayer: Lord, I want to return to You and walk closer. I am not happy with my life. In Jesus' Name, Amen.

JULY 1

Prideful Boasting

2 Kings 20:13 "Hezekiah . . . showed them all the precious things, the silver, and the gold, and the spices."

King Hezekiah brought total strangers into the palace and showed them all the riches of Israel, and it came back to haunt him. They would be motivated to return and take it all. This was God's chastisement for Hezekiah's prideful boasting.

When you are around a crowd of hunters, they pretty soon begin to compare knives, guns, hunting experiences, trucks, and other material things. Then they begin to compare their trophies. They also talk about what famous person they know. All of this is a type of boasting, and even lying, as they try to "outdo" one another. It is caused by pride and indicates a very low self-worth.

Paul tells us in the New Testament that he was happy no matter what condition he was in. A person like that doesn't have to keep on boasting and trying to prove to himself and others how important he is. The Bible says that the persons who continue to "exalt themselves will be abased." (Matthew 23:12)

Prayer: Help me, Lord, not to have to struggle to compete in wealth and fame. Help me be at peace with myself. In Jesus' Name, Amen.

JULY 2

Response to God

2 Kings 22:11 "When the king (Josiah) heard the words of the book of the law, he rent his clothes."

Several years ago, I got shots at two different nice bucks at fairly close range. I don't normally miss at that range, but I did on those two occasions. I learned that my new bifocals weren't compatible with my rifle scope. Anyway, I was sick and embarrassed. I made some changes right away to improve my shooting.

Young King Josiah received the Holy Scriptures that Hilkiah, the priest, had found in the house of God during a renovation project. When they read what the book said, Josiah was terribly grieved because Israel was not following it. If someone tore their clothing, it meant they were really shaken up! A revival took place and Josiah tore down all of the altars of false gods and encouraged everyone to obey God.

How do you respond to preaching, hearing the Bible read, and learning somehow that you have sinned? Some justify themselves, blame others, or condemn the messenger. If we sin, we can only blame ourselves. Do like Josiah, and turn back to God. Others will follow.

Prayer: Make my heart tender, Lord, and help me respond with a broken heart when You speak. In Jesus' Name, Amen.

JULY 3

Good People Die, Too

2 Kings 23:29 "And King Josiah went up against him and he slew him at Megiddo."

My wife's cousin bought a coon dog from a far away state for several hundred dollars. As he was hunting in the wee hours of the morning to try out the dog, the dog struck a trail and was in hot pursuit way out in the middle of nowhere. The branch crossed a paved road, and just as the dog was crossing, a car ran over him - in the middle of the night, in the middle of the road, in the middle of nowhere! What are the chances of that happening?

King Josiah was like no one else in the way he turned his whole heart to God. Yet he went to war to defend his country and was killed by an Egyptian king. It seems to be unjust, doesn't it?

Good people serving good causes die, too, for the strangest reasons. It seems God would protect good people from such tragedy, but He doesn't always. Why? I only know that we serve a loving God and He has a good purpose. We just need to trust His will.

Prayer: Lord, we don't live forever. Help me to be prepared when You are ready for me. In Jesus' Name, Amen.

JULY 4

God Not Defeated

Ezra 1:2 "The Lord God of heaven hath . . . charged me to build Him an house at Jerusalem."

Help comes from unexpected sources sometimes. My dog and I were hunting quail one morning when I heard the sound of beagles barking. I thought, "Oh, no. This won't be a good day." Well, rather than scaring the birds off, they just scattered them all over the woods. My dog pointed some of them one by one and we had a good day.

Cyrus was king of Persia and not likely a true believer in God. He had been commanded by God to rebuild the temple that had been destroyed many years earlier by the Babylonians. The Lord's people were slaves and would not be able to do it by themselves, so God raised up an unbeliever.

People have tried to destroy the Bible and the Christian faith, but it gets stronger. Some have said, "The blood of the saints is the seed of the church." Watch out, for God is in unexpected places, and He can work in spite of bad people and hard circumstances. He will never be defeated by evil or circumstances. Be patient and faithful. He will work it out.

Prayer: Lord, what a great truth! You can't be whipped. Thank You that we are on the winning side. Amen.

JULY 5

Turning Back to God

Ezra 10:1 "When Ezra had prayed . . . there assembled unto him out of Israel a very great congregation of men, women, and children for the people wept very sore."

The coyote problem I mentioned in another devotional was created by another generation, and now we must deal with it. I don't know how to solve it. There are many other wildlife issues that are creating problems. The insurance companies are complaining about so many claims due to deer hitting cars. There are solutions, but we will have to make some changes in our approach to wildlife issues if we want to solve them.

Ezra the priest and many other Israelites had prayed and cried, confessing the sin of the entire nation. They were victims suffering as slaves in Babylon. They didn't create the problem but wanted to return to God and solve it.

There are many problems today that we do not admit creating, such as juvenile crime, drug abuse, illicit sex, etc. We may or may not have created these problems, but we can move in the right direction by turning back to the faith and morality of the Bible to solve these problems and others.

Prayer: Lord, help us to turn back to You. I will change, beginning right now, to be with my kids more and teach other ones to love and obey You as well. Help me. In Jesus' Name, Amen.

JULY 6

Best for the Lord

Nehemiah 2:17 "Ye see the distress that we are in, how Jerusalem lieth in waste."

We have made improvements to my granddaddy's old house for use as a "hunting house." Nothing is painted, and there are a few holes here and there, but it serves our purpose for a place to sleep close to our hunting property. Luxury and beauty are not high priorities. It is kind of refreshing not to worry about things being "just so."

Nehemiah returned from Babylon to see the city of Jerusalem in ruins. It was their place of worship, as well as the capital city of Israel. They could not stand to see it that way, because it was a "black eye" to the people and it dishonored God; therefore, they decided to rebuild.

We should "give of our best to the Master," as the old hymn says. Our houses of worship should look nice, yet many need work. We should honor the Lord with what we wear and how we look when we worship. We don't have to dress in luxury and we should not waste money building extravagant buildings, but we don't need to worship in shorts and let our buildings run down. Provide adequate space, but use God's money wisely to reach people for Christ.

Prayer: Lord, help me to be as concerned about our church building as I am about my house, and as concerned about my dress when I worship as when I go to an important business meeting. In Christ's Name, Amen.

JULY 7

Being Distracted

Nehemiah 6:3 "I cannot come down: why should the work cease?"

Every seasoned turkey hunter knows that it is almost impossible to attract a gobbler away from hens. The gobbler may answer a yelper, but he will not come. If he is by himself, you might call him in.

The enemies of Nehemiah tried every way possible to keep him from rebuilding Jerusalem. They decided that since they couldn't discourage him, they would distract him, which might work just as well. Their plan was to get Nehemiah to leave the work and attend a meeting. They would meet him on the way and kill him. That plan failed when Nehemiah made the statement in our Scripture and refused to go. His job was too important to leave.

A person who is really dedicated to God is hard to distract. There may be things that are really attractive and inviting, but he will not be hindered from doing God's will, since that is his first priority. There is time for wholesome fun, but there are certain times when a Christian must be serving.

Prayer: Block anything, no matter how good it might seem, that would hinder what You want me to do. In Jesus' Name, Amen.

JULY 8

Reverence

Nehemiah 8:5 "And when he opened it (the Word of God), all the people stood up." (Parenthetical comment mine.)

The old house we improved for a "hunting house," as I said, belonged to my granddaddy. I will never forget his reverence for the Lord. As he prayed in church, he turned between the pews and knelt, speaking humbly in a manner that made me realize he knew and deeply respected the One he was talking to.

As Ezra opened the Word of God and read, the people stood from morning until noon and listened with understanding. Afterward, they lifted up their hands and bowed their faces to the ground. What a wonderful time of reverence.

What a special time when people's hearts are tuned to God, and they are seeing Him for who He is and are overwhelmed with adoration and praise.

Prayer: Lord, we worship You with all our hearts. Praise You. Amen.

JULY 9

Time to Act

Esther 4:14 "If thou holdest thy peace then shall . . . deliverance arise to the Jews from another place, but thou and thy father's house shall be destroyed."

There are many things that can wait and are not urgent at all. Whether I hunt today or tomorrow will not likely make much difference. Some may argue that moon phases, weather conditions, etc., matter, and I agree. Really now, it doesn't matter if we get that bird today, does it? It is not an emergency.

There had been a plot to slaughter the Jews, and Queen Esther, a Jew herself, had been told of the plot by her uncle Mordecai. She hesitated to go to the king for deliverance, since she could be killed by the king if she were not invited. In the verse above, Mordecai gives her his warning. She did go to the king, and the Jews were saved.

Other things must be done immediately as well, or all is lost. When a person is having a heart attack or stroke, you must act quickly. Yet other things could be urgent, because time is uncertain. A person could delay confessing his sin and getting his life right with the Lord and get by with it, but maybe not. If you can guarantee you won't die, fine—but you can't. Why run the risk? Anyway, life is much better knowing all is well.

Prayer: Lord, I want to be sure right now that I belong to You and will go to heaven when I die. Forgive me and come into my life. I want to live for You. Thank You. Amen.

JULY 10

When Bad Times Come

Job 1:21 "The Lord gave and the Lord hath taken away; blessed be the name of the Lord."

We hear of all kinds of accidents and tragedies. Hunters accidentally getting shot, deer stands collapsing, people getting bit by rattlesnakes, attacks by wild animals, etc. Where is God in all of this? Job wanted answers, and God gave none. God did not defend Himself. People blame God during these times. He could keep tragedy from happening, and yet He doesn't cause it all to happen. He prevents a great deal from happening that we don't know about.

Job had lost his wealth, his children and his health. His wife was nagging, and his friends blamed it all on him. Job had been a righteous man and did nothing to deserve all of that loss. You would think he would be bitter. His wife said, "Curse God and die." He still was able to say, "Blessed be the name of the Lord."

I am not a pessimist, but we have had bad times, and more maybe are on the way. Some people get through them better than others. It is a matter of spiritual maturity and dependence on the Lord. We should trust Him and have a positive attitude. Above all, we should remember that God is a God of love, and we can always go to Him and leave our burdens there.

Prayer: Lord, I don't know what I will face tomorrow, but I know I can trust You. I am grateful. Amen.

JULY 11

Hard Toward God

Job 9:4 "Who hath hardened himself against Him, and hath prospered?"

Planting food plots for wildlife is a part of our annual routine. Some places we plant have roots, weeds, and a hard crust because they have not been cultivated in many years. If you just put seed and fertilizer out there in those conditions, nothing good will grow. The ground is too hard.

Job makes the point that you can't be hard and argue with God. When Jesus confronted Saul on the road to Damascus, he asked, "Why do you kick against the thorns?" Job says you can't be hard against God and prosper. God is all seeing, all knowing, ever present, all-powerful, and eternal. He has the power of life and death, heaven and hell.

People argue about whether the Bible is true or not, they ignore God, do things they know are wrong, won't go to church, nor read their Bible and pray. That is hardness toward God and it is deadly.

Prayer: God, break our hearts so we will love You and live for You. In Jesus' Name, Amen.

JULY 12

Recorded

Job 16:19 "Behold, my witness is in heaven, and my record is on high."

We keep all kinds of records about trophy game. The only problem is, your name isn't there unless you have earned the right by killing a really large animal. Some people have been left out who have killed some very large deer that were just below the standard.

Job was sitting on an ash heap wearing sacks for clothing, scraping his boils with a piece of wood, and grieving over the loss of his children, wealth and health. His "friends" were still saying that all of this happened to him because he was evil. Job responded by saying that God knows the truth and has it written down. That was all that mattered.

God does have everything written down and we will all have to go before the judgment seat of Christ to give account. We get to heaven by trusting Jesus, and that gets our name put in the "Book of Life," but our rewards are based on what we did with our time, talents, possessions, and opportunities. That is written down, too.

Prayer: Lord, I'm glad my name is written in Your book. Help me fill every page with good works. In Jesus' Name, Amen.

JULY 13

God's Silence

Job 23:3 "Oh that I knew where I might find Him that I might come even to His seat."

Quail hunting, in its peak years, was a lot of pleasure and, at times, was frustrating. We usually found several coveys a day, but there were those days when we just couldn't find them. Whether the dogs just couldn't smell them because of dry weather or sour grass after the first frost, or whether they weren't in their normal places, I don't know. Sometimes, hawks, foxes, bobcats, or other predators would scatter them, and they were in the deep woods.

In all of Job's misery, God didn't seem to be around. There was no improvement in Job's circumstances, even after sincere praying with a pure heart. There were no answers to his questions. Job would have welcomed chastisement or anything just to know God was still around.

Do you ever feel like God is far away? One reason might be unconfessed sin. That wasn't Job's problem, but it often is for us. Another reason is our failure to pray and study God's Word. Another might be that God is giving you time to think and get your heart right. Another is that we have the radio, TV, recreation, or other activities going and aren't listening, or maybe we talk too much and don't listen as we pray.

Prayer: Lord God, help me to be still and know that You are God. In Jesus' Name, Amen.

JULY 14

A Pat on the Back

Job 30:25 "Did not I weep for him that was in trouble and was not my soul grieved for the poor?"

A friend invited me to his old home place for a dove shoot. It was a four hour drive away, but a good shoot is worth it. I was sure that doves would come in, because you never invite people unless there are plenty, and even on the worst day you would get some shots. Well, none, and I mean *none,* came in. I was a little disappointed to say the least. I didn't feel much like patting the man on the back who invited me.

Job was complaining to God that he had done good, cared for the troubled and poor, and went to church, but he was suffering anyway. Rather than being well and happy, he was sick. Job would have preferred that God praise him and make life easy for him since he had been so good.

Praise for a job well done is encouraging, but it should not be expected. Many church people are expecting praise and are mad when they don't get it. Why shouldn't the joy of serving be enough praise for us? Nevertheless, a spouse, people who work for you, your children, and just about anyone is energized by sincere praise. Give plenty of it.

Prayer: Lord, may my service to You bring joy enough that I don't look for praise from people. May I be generous with praise. In Jesus Name, Amen.

JULY 15

God's Answer Comes

Job 38:1 "Then the Lord answered Job out of the whirlwind."

My son-in-law and hunting buddy, Travis, was on the way to our house to pick up my daughter and their two girls to go on vacation. He was overdue and we called him but got no answer. We learned that he had lost his life in a car wreck in a blinding thunderstorm.

I am afraid we believe that God is some heavenly "Santa Claus" or room service who is there to make us happy and do what we want done in our time frame. We ask, "Why doesn't He answer?" Some even wonder if He can answer. Jesus made it clear that He came to "seek and save the lost." The main thing He cares about is souls of all mankind. Though He does meet our needs, it is not his biggest priority that we are free from pain and suffering, have a Perazzi shot gun, or kill a royal elk.

Keep praying and believing. God will mature all of us from the point of wanting things or comfort to wanting Him. He'll knock off some rough edges along the way.

Prayer: May my heart's desire, Lord, be having a closer walk with You and not getting my needs met. In Jesus' Name, Amen.

JULY 16

God's Rebuke

Job 42:8 "Offer up for yourselves a burnt offering and my servant Job shall pray for you."

I believe God hates cruelty and harshness, even to animals. Dog trainers tell of hunters beating their dogs until they won't hunt, and the trainer has a hard time turning the dog around. Any kind of harsh treatment of animals should be avoided. I hate to see deer or other animals suffer when I shoot them. I want to make a quick, clean kill.

God rebuked Job's friends Eliphaz, Bildad, and Zophar, for they had been critical, hurtful, and a curse rather than a blessing to Job. Though at first it appeared that they came to help him, apparently they were jealous of his success, proud of his downfall, and glad to see him suffer.

If God disapproves of harshness to animals, surely he disapproves of harshness to other human beings. It can damage anyone, particularly children. Shouting at others or cutting, critical remarks are never appropriate and are hard to overcome. Sometimes there is a fine line between a parent's sharp chastisement of a child and abuse. There are ways to discipline in kind, definite ways without being harsh.

Prayer: Help me, Lord, to be kind and compassionate with people, gentle in disciplining my children, and even kind to animals. In Jesus' Name, Amen.

JULY 17

A Comeback

Job 42:10 "And the Lord turned the captivity of Job, when he prayed for his friends."

Job's trials were over. He maintained a good attitude and refused to curse and turn his back on God. He prayed for his friends, even after the hard things they had said about him. Job received twice as much material goods and family as he had before, as well as his health. God allowed Satan to go just so far in his testing of Job.

People lose their jobs, experience a divorce, become sick, lose family members and many other things dear to them, and think it is over and that they can't go on. Our state of mind can get so low that we get depressed. Don't think about how bad things are when that happens to you. Think of what a mighty God we serve. Don't think of what you cannot do. God can send someone along or change your circumstances. Keep praying, hanging on, and doing all you can to change things. God will break through.

Somebody gave my in-laws a little dog that they really didn't want. It wasn't long before my father-in-law died. The little dog meant so much to my mother-in-law who was living alone. God saw what she would need and took care of it. It didn't heal everything, but it sure made things easier. God will do it for you.

Prayer: Lord, thank You that when things go bad, you are still there and can bring me back. Thanks again. Amen.

JULY 18

A Father's Dream

Job 42:16 "After this lived Job an hundred and forty years and saw his sons and his son's sons, even four generations."

It is a thrilling thing to see your bird dog loping around the edge of a field, slow down to a walk, and then freeze with a foot up and his head and tail high. That is the prettiest thing in sports to me. Another great thrill is flushing the birds, pulling the trigger twice, and watching two birds tumble from the sky.

The book of Job begins in tragedy, heartache, and suffering. It ends with a grand climax, picturing Job and four generations by his side. There is a great deal of love and harmony implied. That would be a daddy's dream-come-true. A united family filled with love and mutual respect, and, in addition, all of them trusting in Jesus and serving Him.

Too often that doesn't happen because of family breakups, but you can make a new start, though a marriage might not be reunited. Be at peace in your heart with the former mate and forgive. Hold no grudges. Get closer to your current spouse and children. Confess any sin and begin serving the Lord. At the end of your life, your dream may come true.

Prayer: Lord, give us a better family than ever, and help me lead so that we will love each other until the end. In Jesus' Name, Amen.

JULY 19

True Happiness

Psalm 1:1 "Blessed is the man that walketh not in the counsel of the ungodly not standeth in the way of sinners, not sitteth in the seat of the scornful."

Everyone is looking for happiness. It makes some of us happy to be out in the woods behind a dog, up a deer stand, or in a duck blind. That is all so relaxing and peaceful to me. You don't have a worry in the world, and you are with family and friends. The game you might get is "icing on the cake."

Though that is true, when you have to come back to the real world, the problems and responsibilities are still there. Hunting can be a temporary escape, but I want something that lasts and that makes me feel secure all the time.

Psalm 1 tells us that the answer is living a godly life. It says that the ungodly are like trash blowing around, and that they cannot stand up to God's judgment and will perish spiritually. God knows His people by name, and they will last forever.

Prayer: Lord, help me to live a godly life and find true happiness. In Jesus' Name, Amen.

JULY 20

A Shield

Psalm 3:3 "Thou, O Lord, art a shield for me."

How many times have I heard bow hunters talk about missing deer because of a tiny limb or stem that deflected their arrow? The arrow was on target until it suddenly veered to one side, and the spooked animal bounded off. The stick served as a protective shield for him.

The psalmist had "troubles" in large numbers, and people were saying, "There is no help for him in God." David wrote this psalm when Absalom, his son, was trying to kill him and take the throne. David was able to sleep at night because he knew the Lord was protecting him.

Many of us have fears, doubts, and anxiety about things going on in our lives, such as health, job, terrorism, the economy, our children, aging parents, and money. This is all in spite of the fact that we have been responsible and done all we can. Remember this: The things we can't control must be turned over to the Lord. God is our shield.

Prayer: Lord, I can rest just knowing that when I do my best, Your shield protects me. Thank You. Amen.

JULY 21

Trust

Psalm 7:1 "O Lord my God, in thee do I put my trust."

Who can you trust? People let us down at times. They make promises they don't keep. We loan friends our tools, and they never bring them back. The service station changes the oil in your car and forgets to put any back in. A friend was given a bird dog that he had to pay to be shipped across the country and the dog turned out to be vicious. He would bite you if he could.

In this psalm, David, called upon the Lord because of people who persecuted him without cause. He did not mention calling on family and friends for help, because he didn't know if they could be trusted. He knew that he could trust God, so he called on Him.

Are you a trustworthy family member or friend? Do they suspect that you lie to them? Is other people's money safe around you when they are not looking? Do you pay your bills on time? Can your wife trust you? Do you trust God, or do you trust your money, health, power, and intelligence? Some day they will not be enough. Trust God.

Prayer: I am trusting in You. Help me trust You more. In Jesus' Name, Amen.

JULY 22

Unworthiness

Psalm 8:4 "What is man that thou art mindful of him?"

David was a shepherd in his early days and had lots of time to look at God's creation as he tended his father's sheep. He could see the birds, craggy mountains, and winding streams. He could smell the fragrance of flowers as he was blessed by their beauty. He viewed the spectacular night sky with millions of stars and heavenly bodies floating by.

I feel the same way as I sit in a tree before daylight and then see the sunrise awaken the sparkling dew. The sky seems to go on forever. Then a squirrel rustles the leaves as he searches for food. Once a sparrow lit on my gun barrel as I sat camouflaged and motionless. It all makes you very humble.

We are unworthy, you know, not only to experience those things, but it really comes home to us as we realize that "while we were yet sinners, Christ died for us."

Prayer: Lord, all I can say is thank You. Amen.

JULY 23

Fruit of Seeking

Psalm 9:10 "For thou, Lord, hast not forsaken them that seek Thee."

One Thanksgiving morning, a shot rang out from the direction of my daughter, Dawn's, deer stand. We began our search for the deer based on a little spot of blood. We weren't sure which trail he took or if it was a death hit. We interrupted the search for the big lunch at my mother and dad's, and when we resumed, we finally found her nice six point stone dead in the creek. We almost gave up at times but finally had success.

David had plenty of experiences to draw from as background to praising God for His justice and faithfulness–running from Saul and Absalom, fighting all of his wars, and being king. There were many times and many different reasons he had to count on God, and he always found Him there.

God is not hard to find when we go about it in the right way. He is not running from us or playing hard to get. He desperately wants a relationship with us. Jeremiah 29:13 says, "You shall find me if you seek me with all your heart." You can't do that living your way. It doesn't mean a frantic, exhausting search but surrendering to His way and forsaking yours.

Prayer: Lord, help me to not just claim I want a relationship with You. Help me to just give up and follow. In Jesus' Name, Amen.

JULY 24

Forsaken

Psalm 22:1 "My God, my God why hast Thou forsaken me?"

When I was a very small boy, maybe three or four, the older boys, who were four to eight years older, would take the coon dogs with daddy and go out at night to hunt. It would have been hard at that age tearing through the briars and vines and crossing creeks in the dark, but I still wanted to go and really felt left out when I couldn't.

This psalm is a cry out to God by David in his distress. He felt that God had abandoned him to his enemies. Jesus uttered those same words from the cross. The Father could not look upon sin and turned His back, so to speak, on the Son as He took our load of sin upon Himself.

You might feel forsaken or lonely. Maybe your spouse left you or died. Maybe your children have moved away from home and you have an empty nest. Maybe some friend or loved one is no longer near, temporarily or permanently. Maybe you even feel that God has forsaken you. Take heart! He hasn't moved. Have you? Draw near to Him and He will comfort you.

Prayer: Lord, I know You are near, even if dear ones are not. I will draw comfort from Your presence. Thank You. Amen.

JULY 25

Being Followed Around

Psalm 23:6 "Surely goodness and mercy shall follow me all the days of my life."

In my early days, as I would get up and out way before daylight and go into the woods, I would feel that some evil thing was following me. Have you ever felt that way? A panther, coyote, or something could be creeping up behind me. It made me want to get up my stand in a hurry.

David spoke of the Lord being his shepherd, meeting all of his needs, leading him in righteousness, and picking him up when he was down. He gave him victory over his enemies. David believed that goodness and mercy were following him around.

What is following you around? There was a cartoon character that had a cloud over his head and rain on his face all of the time. Are bad things following you around, or good things? If it is bad, try changing your focus to good and godly things and people. Good will begin to follow you.

Prayer: God, I want to change my life for the better and cause better things to happen to me and my family. Help me accept what I cannot change and follow You more closely. In Jesus' Name, Amen.

JULY 26

God's Secrets

Psalm 25:14 "The secret of the Lord is with them that fear Him; and He will show them His covenant."

Hunters that want to be successful must know some of the "secrets" of the game they are hunting. Where do they go at night? What spooks them and attracts them—noises, smells, and foods? When are they active and what are their patterns? How well can they see and what colors are they sensitive to?

This verse talks about God's secrets. This does not mean that He intentionally keeps things from certain people. He does not have favorites, but he does have intimates. He is close and reveals more of Himself and His truth to some than others. It makes a difference how close we are to Him.

I hate to see people whispering in public, apparently telling secrets they only want a few to hear, particularly when they smirk and snicker. That is bad manners. God will let anyone know Him if he prays, reads His Word, and lives an obedient life, no matter how rich or poor, old or young, or what his background has been.

Prayer: Lord, what a thought! I can really know You and be close to You. Thank You. Amen.

JULY 27

Forgiven

Psalm 32:1 "Blessed is he whose transgression is forgiven."

Hunting, in a way, is a very unforgiving sport. When I was about twelve years old, I had never hunted ducks much, and I got a new single barrel twelve gage with a thirty inch full choke barrel for Christmas. I still have it. We went down to a pond close by our house early one morning. A big green headed mallard came whistling by. I shot and missed him, "cold turkey." There I was with my empty gun, helplessly watching him fly away, never to be seen again. There was no other chance at him for me.

Psalm 32 is David's feeling after he confessed his affair with Bathsheba and the sin of killing her husband. His burden was lifted, and he would not be held accountable to God. Even his body ached before he confessed, but then God forgave him and his burden disappeared.

People hold grudges against us and won't forgive. God is not like that, and there is no sin—not even rape, murder, stealing, divorce, or anything else—that God will not forgive. You can't think of one that you have done that He will not forgive if you turn away from it and turn to Him and ask.

Prayer: What a blessing, Lord, that I don't have to live with guilt and regret. Thank You. Amen.

JULY 28

Godly Nation

Psalm 33:12 "Blessed is the nation whose God is the Lord."

A tremendous amount of time and money is spent these days on sports and recreation. Even low income hunters think nothing of spending hundreds of dollars on guns, dogs, clothes, boots, guides, and travel expenses for hunting. I am not concerned about some money being spent for things like that. I do it myself, but we have gone overboard.

Is that a sign that we are in trouble? Over and above what we spend on hunting, there is time and money spent on golf, spectator sports, makeup for women, and extravagant clothing, cars, and houses. Maybe that is okay. Some nice things and recreation are fine, but who is our God in America?

With children killing children, a high divorce rate, crime, unwed pregnancies, and corruption among high officials, you wonder if our sports is not a symptom of our god being SELF rather than God. The Word says, "Blessed (happy) is the nation whose God is the Lord." Maybe we need to do some soul searching. If not, we will wreck our homes and nation.

Prayer: Lord, our nation is in a mess. Help us to turn back to You. In Jesus' Name, Amen.

JULY 29

Teaching Children

Psalm 34:11 "Come, ye children, hearken unto me: I will teach you the fear of the Lord."

Young bird dog puppies from good blood lines will point as soon as they can walk. Take a fishing pole and tie a bird wing to a string, or even a rag, and the whole litter will lock down on it. They have to be trained, though, in several ways: pointing quail only, not flushing birds before the hunter gets there, not eating the birds you shoot, and taking dead birds to the one who shot them. Also, they should honor another dog's point.

The writer of this psalm knew who he would teach and what he would teach them. He knew that children had to be taught what you want them to know. If not, you run the risk of others teaching them what they want them to know. They aren't born knowing what is right. We can't just expect them to watch our example and know what to do. They misinterpret that and learn bad habits.

What are you teaching your children, dad? You are being held accountable by God to teach them. Take them to church, read the Bible and pray with them, live a godly life, and above all, teach them how the Bible applies to life.

Prayer: Lord, I have only a short time to train my children. That door opens and closes fast. Help me, and I will do it. In Jesus' Name, Amen.

JULY 30

God Listens

Psalm 34:15 "The eyes of the Lord are on the righteous,
and his ears are open unto their cry."

Some of us wonder if God is really out there or if He cares. There are billions of people in the world, and maybe a couple billion are Christians. Does the Bible mean that He sees and hears every one of us all of the time? Yes, God is all-seeing and all-knowing. That is hard for us to understand.

Hunting doves is a challenge. They fly so many different speeds and come from so many different directions until it is hard to adjust and lead them the right amount. They can fly behind you and be out of range before you know it. You just can't look in every direction at the same time, but God does.

We judge God, too often, by our limitations. We feel that He is just as limited as we are. I can only think of one person at a time. He hears the righteous people all at one time and begins to meet their needs according to His will.

Prayer: Lord, You are a loving and mighty God. I can't understand how You hear us all at one time, but I know that You do. Thank You. Amen.

JULY 31

Evil for Good

Psalm 35:12 "They rewarded me evil for good."

That is the way things work sometime. My brother, Bill, caught a red bird (cardinal) in a trap when I was a little boy, and all I wanted to do was pet him, but he pecked me. He thought we wanted to harm him, because he lived in an environment where he could be caught and eaten.

David had apparently done something good for someone, and they misinterpreted it and did evil for good. Once, he sent some men to comfort the son of a friend who had died, and the son shaved off their beards and cut off their shirt tails, humiliating them.

Jesus turned all of that around and said, "Love your enemies. Do good to them that hate you." That is so different from human nature, but there is a good feeling about it, and it's God's will.

Prayer: Lord, it's so hard to be like You and do good for evil. I'm willing. You do it through me. Amen.

AUGUST 1

Doing Right

Psalm 37:1 "Fret not thyself because of evil doers."

It has always bothered me a great deal when I hear of people trapping whole coveys of quail, hunting deer with spotlights at night, and other illegal things without ever getting caught.

This psalm of David laments the same problem. Sometimes people seem to even prosper by mistreating others and being dishonest. However, David says in the verse after ours, "They shall be cut down like the grass and wither as the green herb." God is watching, justice will be done, and every wrong made right.

Honesty and playing by the rules pays off. A good Christian testimony and sound reputation is a powerful influence to family and associates. I don't want to have to go around feeling guilty or worrying about whether the law is going to catch me or not. Better still, I want to be approved in the eyes of God by doing right.

Prayer: Lord, I commit to do right all day, every day, for Your glory. In Jesus' Name, Amen.

AUGUST 2

God's Blessing

Psalm 37:4 "Delight thyself also in the Lord, and He will give you the desires of your heart."

That is quite a promise. Believers who delight in putting God first will be given the things that really satisfy them most. He made us and knows what really satisfies our souls.

Hunters who try to get satisfaction and joy out of just sports are never satisfied. They kill a big deer and somebody kills a bigger one. The satisfaction of it soon goes away. I know many people who have burned out on hunting and keep looking for something else to excite them, but it is all temporary.

Life is short and things that make us feel good now will end. God will never disappoint us. As we honor Him with our lives and serve Him, the joy comes permanently. So many times, He has given us things that we never asked for that blessed our lives, all because we try to serve Him.

Prayer: Lord, I confess I have delighted in so many things that don't satisfy. Help me put my focus on You. In Jesus' Name, Amen.

AUGUST 3

A Bad Temper

Psalm 37:8 "Cease from anger."

Have you ever noticed that some people get mad at the "drop of a hat." If things don't go their way on the hunt, their dog isn't hunting well, they miss a few shots, and then they really get steamed. They are touchy, the least little thing sets them off, and they stay mad a long time. I have been guilty of that.

"Cease from anger" means don't get mad easily and then don't stay mad. It is a sign of selfishness or impatience, and it displeases God. Jesus got mad in the temple and turned over the tables of the money changers because they were dishonoring the Lord's house and cheating people. His anger was not selfish.

A family, church, business, or anything else runs better when people are not cranky. It is a good testimony for people to enjoy being around you, and yet they surely won't if you have a bad temper.

Prayer: Lord, getting angry hurts me and others. Help me not to be so easily upset. In Jesus' Name, Amen.

AUGUST 4

Burdens

Psalm 55:22 "Cast thy burden upon the Lord and He shall sustain thee."

Have you ever killed a deer way off the trail in a watery swamp and had to drag it out by yourself? You are trying to drag him by his horns and your boots are bogging down and slipping. When you get out, you are cold, wet, and bloody. It will wear you out!

The Lord knew we would have burdens of another type–worries. They are things we can't control that are too heavy to bear alone. If there are things we neglect or problems we can correct, we should, but we worry about other burdens that should be left in God's hands.

People all around us have burdens. Help them if you can. Listen to their problems, and be an encourager. Remind them that we can lay our burdens on the Lord. Pray with them.

Prayer: Lord, I have burdens I cannot bear alone. I lay them on You. I will be responsible by doing all I can to lift them. Thank You. Amen.

AUGUST 5

On My Side

Psalm 56:9 "God is for me."

So many times, God is thought of as a great big man with a skinning knife ready to take off our hide with a great deal of pleasure when we fail. He disciplines His children when He needs to, because he loves us. He is on our side.

When we used to discipline our children, we constantly assured them, "We are on your side. We are not the enemy." They thought we were against them, but we only wanted to help them do what was best.

Everything God does is because of His love for us, even when He allows us to go through bad times. We should all do things with love, from responding to unkind people to correcting our own children. That communicates that we are on their side.

Prayer: Lord, help me to know You are on my side, even when You chastise me. In Jesus' Name, Amen.

AUGUST 6

Fool

Psalm 53:1 "The fool has said in his heart there is no God."

Have you ever noticed how many different species of animals, birds, reptiles, flowers, trees, and other living things there are? Look around sometime when you are walking in the woods or just sitting in a stand. There must be tens of thousands. Someone told me how many different kinds of spiders there are. It was in the hundreds. Did all of this evolve from one cell? If so, it looks like to me there would be only one or two species. Did it all come from some giant explosion? Scientists now are discounting that more and more and talking about "intelligent design." Even secular scientists are talking about some creator. We call Him God.

You may say, "I believe there is a God." Some people say they do and live like they don't. That is what David was saying in the psalm when he says, "in his heart." Down deep, this kind of person really doesn't believe, because we live what we believe.

Do you show you believe by your language, habits, the way you treat your family, your character, and the time you spend thinking about God, or do your associates wonder about you? It is true that "we arc the only Jesus some will ever know."

Prayer: Help me show others that God is in my life so that they do not act foolishly and deny You. In Jesus' Name, Amen.

AUGUST 7

Waiting on God

Psalm 62:1 "Truly my soul waiteth upon God."

David waits on God to save him, defend him, and give him strength in this psalm. He says, "I shall not be greatly moved," which means people and circumstances will not hinder or destroy him if he obeys God at the right time. Things happen in God's time, not man's. Sometimes waiting is necessary.

Regularly, I hear of turkey hunters who call but get no response. Some have just sat still and waited, then suddenly, a big gobbler moves quietly in sight. Others have given up and decided to move, only to see the backside of one with a twenty-seven inch beard flying out of range!

Sometimes, God doesn't operate in our time frame. We are praying and doing all we can, but nothing seems to happen. Don't act impulsively, as I have at times. Wait until you sense God saying, "Now is the time to act." Timing is important, as well as action. Even what is right is wrong when the timing is not God's.

Prayer: Help me to know when to wait and when to act. Thank You. Amen.

AUGUST 8

Shooting Bows

Psalm 64:7 "God shall shoot at them with an arrow."

Almost every year, my son Boyd shoots a deer with his bow and arrow. That thing is lethal at close range. The point and blades are razor sharp and when launched from a seventy or so pound pull, they pack a wallop. Usually, the animal falls pretty close to where he is hit.

David tells of how the wicked counsel against him is like a sword, and their bitter words are like arrows from a bow. The wicked person acts secretly, like an arrow as it slips through the air without a whisper, expecting that no one will know. However, God will shoot the wicked with an arrow and wound them.

The world is full of people who love to find some little tidbit of gossip and spread it. Don't worry about that. God's bow is at full draw. Also, watch out concerning your own sharp tongue and unkind words about others. You will find God's arrow stuck up to the feathers in you!

Prayer: Lord, protect me from the arrows of my enemy. In Jesus' Name, Amen.

AUGUST 9

Mercy

Psalm 67:1 "God be merciful unto us and bless us."

Probably every deer hunter has set in his deer stand early in the morning with his scope on a doe, or even a respectable buck, mulling over whether to squeeze off a round or not. The thought in mind is that if you do, you might spook a Boone and Crocket. Not shooting probably could not be called an "act of mercy."

In this psalm, David is praying for God's mercy and blessing. God is certainly capable of granting that request of a godly person. His answer will be based on what is best in the long run and not on self interest, like the hunter who didn't shoot.

Mercy is what we need, for if we got what we deserve, we would all be in trouble. When we pray for mercy, we are asking God to control things and not let us be at the mercy of people and circumstances. It is far better to entrust ourselves to His care.

Prayer: Lord, I feel good to be at Your mercy, because I know You love me and want my best. Thank You. Amen.

AUGUST 10

Waters in the Soul

Psalm 69:1 "Save me, O God, for the waters are come unto my soul."

My son and I were riding in the deep woods one wet spring when the little creeks and branches were full of water. We were in our 1976 Ford Bronco with four wheel drive, so we felt pretty secure. On those models, you had to get out and manually turn the hubs on the front wheels to engage four wheel drive. We began to spin, so I got out and turned them, but it was too late. My tires were slick, and we were soon bogged down up to the doors and had to be rescued by a man on a tractor.

Life had gotten the best of David, and he compared it to deep waters. He called out to God, because he was deluged by the flood and tired of crying. Before God's answer came, he began to give thanks and praised God. He knew God would hear him.

It is true that it is "hard to drain the swamp when you're up to your eyes in alligators." "Waters in the soul" can be caused by sin, depression, or troubles of many kinds. The answer for all of it is to call out to God and know that He will save you.

Prayer: Sometimes, Lord, life is too hard for me. Lift me out of the mud hole that I am in. In Jesus Name, Amen.

AUGUST 11

Praying for Leadership

Psalm 72:1 "Give the king thy judgments, O God, and thy righteousness unto the king's son."

Here David is praying for his son, Solomon, who would soon be the king of Israel. The prayer is for justice for the poor and needy, for prosperity, and submission of other kingdoms to his authority.

We are encouraged to pray for people in authority, that they rule well. Paul, in the New Testament, was under cruel rule of the Romans, but he still encouraged submission, unless leadership called on them to disobey God. Change in a nation should be made through elections and other peaceful means. Christians should always vote, and some should run for office. There is a need for leaders in government and elsewhere who have integrity.

Pray for those who make hunting laws and decisions about the environment. Hunters are also, or should be, good citizens and supportive of good leadership.

Prayer: I pray for our leaders, that they take note of the down and out. Help me to be a better, more active citizen. For Your sake, Amen.

AUGUST 12

Thankfulness

Psalm 75:1 "Unto thee, O God, do we give thanks."

When the psalmist says this, he acknowledges that God has blessed him with many good things, but more than that, he gives thanks for God Himself. He responds to God's goodness by pledging to follow His will.

Hunters, of all people, have been blessed generously. I suppose we enjoy more of nature than anyone, and under all conditions—from the cold of winter, when some birds have gone and others have come, to the heat of summer, when the flowers are in bloom. Proud does wander about with their spotted fawns, and quail chase bugs for their tiny brood.

I love nature, but I do not worship it. It makes me think of our Creator who made it all, and I want to bow my heart and say, "Thank You." Then I want to show what I feel by serving Him.

Prayer: Lord, thank You, thank You. Amen.

AUGUST 13

Songs in the Night

Psalm 77:6 "I call to remembrance my song in the night."

There are not many birds that sing at night. I love to hear the whippoorwill in April, when they arrive here. The great horned owl can make a cry that will cause the hair to raise up on your neck. Sometimes you can hear a mockingbird, but other than that, the birds are silent until very early in the morning.

The psalmist is in a time of great distress and remembers a song in the night. It was not the song of a bird, but his own song that he sang for joy at an unusual time when he should be asleep—the middle of the night.

That is a good idea. When the days are filled with pain, fear, and doubt, remember the good times. Focus on good, not bad; joy, not sorrow; and happiness, not sadness. Think back to a time when your heart was singing, then think of the Lord, the author of all good songs.

Prayer: There are dark times when I need a song, Lord. Help me to remember the good times and sing again. In Jesus' Name, Amen.

AUGUST 14

Reloading

Psalm 85:5 "Wilt thou be angry with us forever?"

Israel had sinned against God; they repented and wondered if He would continue to hold it against them. They wanted to be placed back in His favor as they were before. The land was suffering, and crops weren't growing. God had withdrawn His blessing. God promised to restore them.

Some hunters reload their own ammunition. I used to reload shotgun shells for my own use with a hand loader. I would pick up hulls at dove shoots from expensive shells, and they worked fine. The brass on cheap shells would expand and jam my automatic. You could put the amount of powder and size shot in the reloaded shell and make a better shell than it was before.

Like shotgun shells, we can be spent and feel empty because we let ourselves become too much like the world and drift into sin. God hates that and has provided a way to make things right again. His "anger" doesn't have to last forever, and we can confess, forsake our sin, and be good as new.

Prayer: Lord, I know you hate some things I do. I hate it, too, but I struggle at times. I want to reload. I'll try to do better. Forgive me. Thank You. Amen

AUGUST 15

Learning His Way

Psalm 86:11 "Teach me thy way, O Lord, I will walk in thy truth."

Shooting quail on the covey rise is one of the most exciting and challenging things in sports. They suddenly get up, scare you to death, and before you recover, they are out of range. Now I know how you do it. Be calm, pick out one bird at a time, and lead him just right. That is easier said than done.

Our verse is a promise to God to learn and follow through. Further, the writer asks God to help him "fear His name." It does take a type of fear or respect for God to obey what we know. God, I believe, only reveals His truth to those who plan to follow.

Some people, like I do with shooting quail, know what to do but don't do it. With hunting, I have the will, but fail to pull it off. God will help us to obey if we only have the will to learn His way.

Prayer: Lord, I want to substitute Your will for mine in every situation from now on, so teach me Your way. In Jesus' Name, Amen.

AUGUST 16

God is Forever

Psalm 90:2 "Even from everlasting to everlasting, thou art God."

Hunting trips just don't last long enough. It seems that by the time you get started, it is time to go. You try to make it last longer by talking about it over and over. If I didn't prefer to be with my wife and children, I would live in the woods all the time.

A hunting trip ends, but God is forever. He was not created, so He has always been. He is unique because everything and everyone else had a beginning and was created by Him.

God doesn't need anything, but He created us out of love and for us to love Him. We will also live with Him forever.

Prayer: Lord, You are eternal, and I know that my spirit will live forever because Christians die and rise again. It humbles me. Amen.

AUGUST 17

The Vision of God

Psalm 90:4 "For a thousand years in thy sight are but as yesterday."

Human beings are limited in ways that God is not. I think I can remember some things when I was a year or so old. I know I remember hunting sparrows with a bb gun and trying to get a robin with my 22 rifle as I grew older. However, I know nothing about what will happen tomorrow.

God is different. To God, a thousand years in the future is as clear as the past. He, at this moment, is seeing past, present, and future all at one time. We call that "omniscience." That is the reason He can know what is going to happen in advance and try to prepare us for it. He lets us have free will so that we will choose to love Him.

God's Word, His Holy Spirit, others, and experience can prepare us for the unknown. Since His vision to the future is perfect, it is important for us to let Him guide us. Someone standing at the top of a hill can see two cars coming from different directions on the same side of the road and warn them. God sees everything in the future and we can avoid disaster if we listen to Him.

Prayer: Lord, help my mind be open to Your will that I may use Your perfect vision. In Jesus' Name, Amen.

AUGUST 18

Life Is Short

Psalm 90:10 "The days of our years are threescore years and ten."

The verse continues and says that if we are strong, life may be eighty rather than seventy (a score is twenty years). This is not a promise from God, but an observation. Some die as babies and others reach one hundred, but these days, life expectancy for men is about seventy and for women, maybe seventy eight.

Elephants can live to be over one hundred years old. Deer probably live about ten years, and your old bird dog may live to be twelve or fourteen if he doesn't get heart worms. Life is short for every living thing. Animals have no knowledge of eternity, because when they die, that is it. It is different for humans, because we are created in God's image.

The spirit of man lives forever, though life on this planet is short. This is simple preparation for the long, long life after this one. I want to spend it in a perfect place with God and perfect people, don't you?

Prayer: Lord, help me to live everyday as though it were my last. In Jesus' Name, Amen.

AUGUST 19

Every Day Counts

Psalm 90:12 "Teach us to number our days, that we may apply our hearts to wisdom."

Early in the morning, in my experience, is the best time to hunt most any kind of game–very early for some types. Time of day really matters. Wanting to be with my family a certain morning, I stayed around the house and didn't get out very early. I went later and hunted during the middle of the day, but got no response from even one lovesick gobbler. A neighbor near where I hunt said, "Yeah, I heard some gobble over there on your place real early."

When you hunt is important, but "counting your days" is more so. Every day is important. The psalm says, "that we may apply our hearts to wisdom." Living wisely means making every minute count. Every day we do not live for the Lord is wasted.

The careers we select should bring honor to Christ and be beneficial in serving others. Producing and selling alcohol and tobacco products are damaging. Free time should not be spent gambling and reading pornography. Watching TV programming that is crude and sexually arousing is a waste of time. Fill your mind at work or at leisure with thoughts of what is good. Every day counts.

Prayer: Lord, help me fill every day with thoughts and deeds that honor You, so that every day counts. In Jesus' Name, Amen.

AUGUST 20

In Charge

Psalm 93:1 "The Lord reigneth, He is clothed with majesty."

I have hunted elk once or twice and know little about it. Pictures I see and what I have heard indicate that the big bull is there protecting the cows. His large body and antlers serve as a warning to predators and inferior bulls, which assures the future of the herd.

It seems that evil is going to win out at times. People seem to get worse in their moral behavior, meanness, and dishonest ways. The devil seems to have free reign. Is he in charge? No, God gives people a will to choose, and He wants us to choose good. He will let things go so far and then set us straight.

Does it really pay off to love the Lord and live right? God has His natural law in this life. Sexual license has brought on unwanted pregnancies, crippling and deadly diseases, and destruction of homes. Tobacco can kill you. In the next life, all wrongs will be made right. Unbelievers go to hell, and believers can lose their rewards. The Lord reigns forever and forever.

Prayer: Lord, I trust You to show Your might when You want to. Thank You that You are in charge. In Jesus' Name, Amen.

AUGUST 21

Singing to the Lord

Psalm 100:1 "Make a joyful noise unto the Lord."

One of the best things about being in the woods and fields to me is hearing the birds. There is the cheerful "peep" of robins, the comforting chirp from martins, or a variety of songs from a mockingbird. They can be a great deal of company when you are sitting there by yourself.

God has invited us to make a "joyful noise" unto Him. We might think our song is just noise, and we might not be able to carry a tune, but everyone has been given a song by the Lord. It lifts the spirits of people who hear you just singing as you go. You don't have to sing in a choir, but sing.

My grandpa Green used to sing a lot while he was out in the fields by himself farming. "I Shall Not Be Moved" was one of his favorites. He didn't have a great voice. My Uncle Tommie told how he enjoyed Grandpa's singing. God loves it, others are encouraged by it, and it will bless you.

Prayer: Lord, I want to sing more, not for me, but for Your glory. In Jesus Name, Amen.

AUGUST 22

Say So

Psalm 107:2 "Let the redeemed of the Lord say so."

Several of the psalms say, "bless the Lord," or "give thanks to the Lord," and give reasons why He is worthy of it. It is the purest form of worship when we begin to tell the Lord we love Him and how He has blessed us. It honors Him and we are blessed, too.

A good time to praise God is when you are out in the woods. Focus your mind on the Lord rather than secular things you could think about. Begin to remember His blessings—health, family, a free country, plenty, etc.

One of the best ways to bless the Lord is to tell others about Jesus. Tell them how you used to live and what caused you to change, but mostly, how Christ has made a difference in you. Are you saved? Say so in a loving, sensitive way.

Prayer: Lord, it is hard to tell others about You, but give me the power to do it. For Jesus' sake, Amen.

AUGUST 23

An Ounce of Prevention

Psalm 119:11 "Thy word have I hid in my heart, that I might not sin against thee."

As we were getting ready to go on an elk hunt out west, we knew we had to really be well prepared. The terrain is rough, and the altitude is high, so we had to be in top physical condition. We knew that if we saw an elk, he would be a long way off, so we bought the right kind of bullets, zeroed our rifles, and practiced over and over again. You can't afford to miss a shot because you will not likely get another chance.

As we try to be obedient Christians, we have to put as much as possible in our favor. We need to know God's Word and be motivated. One of the best ways to do that is studying the Bible and memorizing portions. Today's verse says we should hide the word in our heart so that when temptation comes, we will recognize it for what it is and resist. Many disobey because of ignorance.

You can prevent a lot of problems and mistakes in life by spending the time to learn God's ways. The best place to find out His ways is in His Word. Prepare yourself for the battle of everyday life.

Prayer: Lord, I commit to study Your Word more. Help me to learn and understand it. In Jesus' Name, Amen.

AUGUST 24

The Last Word

Psalm 119:89 "Forever, O Lord, thy word is settled in heaven."

There are lots of opinions out there about scents to use for deer hunting. Some use doe scents, buck scents, fox scents, scents of dirt, apples, and you name it. I don't know who is right. I guess it is according to whether the rut is on or not. I can't be sure any of them have consistently worked for me.

Opinions don't count with God. His truth is what counts. People are ready to tell you what they believe about God. Some believe things because some friend or family member said it. We seem to think we are going to get by with practicing what we believe to be true. Opinions vary as to how to live and who God is. The matter is settled in heaven and is not up for debate.

Don't count on what someone else's opinion is. Learn for yourself. What is written in the Bible has been approved by God in heaven, and it will never change. It is the last word and explains how we will be judged.

Prayer: The last word was uttered by You, Lord, on the cross—"It is finished." I believe it. Amen.

AUGUST 25

Value of Trials

Psalm 119:71 "It is good for me that I have been afflicted, that I might learn Thy statutes."

Every kind of wildlife has keen senses in order to survive. Turkeys and hawks have very keen eyesight. Deer have blinding speed and an incredible sense of smell. Rattlesnakes can sense movement and warmth that most animals can't. God made them that way because it is a matter of life and death, and they struggle to make their senses better. I am told that people who lose one of their senses become sharper in one or all of their others.

How can the psalmist say it is good that he suffered? People become stronger when they have to struggle with something. When muscles are exercised they become stronger, and the same is true of the mind. There was a saying about the early church, "The blood of the martyrs was the seed of the church." Many were being killed for their faith, but Christianity grew in spite of it.

I don't know what hard things you might be going through now or what you will go through in the future. If you respond with the right attitude, you will be stronger. That is why God allows it.

Prayer: Lord, I will gladly go through what I must to be more like You. Thank You. Amen.

AUGUST 26

With God's Help

Psalm 127:1 "Except the Lord build the house, they labor in vain that build it."

Getting up early to go hunting requires an alarm clock for me much of the time. I would probably just sleep on until six o'clock without one. Have you ever thought of a clock with no hands? The first thing that comes to my mind is "worthless."

The verse you just read (and the rest of the psalm that follows) talks about building, protecting, finding bread, etc., without the Lord. That is like a clock without hands. It just goes around and around but doesn't do any good. God expects our best efforts, but without Him, we fail.

Also, a life without God's help is the same way. We need His protection, blessing, and guidance. He works in our lives and circumstances when we are not aware of it as we allow Him. Invite Him in, and keep your eyes open to see Him come along side of you.

Prayer: Lord, thank you for being that strength, that extra hand, that force we need every day to make our home a home and our lives complete. In Jesus' Name, Amen.

AUGUST 27

Space

Psalm 132:6 "We found it in the fields of the wood."

David was looking for a place where he could find God. The hardships of life had overcome him, and he was looking for rest and strength to go on. He was so desperate that he vowed not to sleep until he found Him (God). He heard that God was in Bethlehem, but he found Him in the woods.

Game will put as much space as possible between them and their enemies, which are primarily predators. Quail fly to their roost so that they don't leave a trail. Deer retreat to secure, secluded areas when hunting pressure comes.

People need space as well. Children in cities get into so much trouble because they keep bumping into people and things when they are expending their energy. They need to get out in the woods and wide open spaces so they can run, jump, and scream without offending anyone. They hear "be still and be quiet" too often. If you can, get the family out in the open woods often. If not, fence in a large area and give them freedom to unwind.

Prayer: God, sometimes I need to get away and feel free. So often, that is when I find You. Thank You. Amen.

AUGUST 28

Away From Home

Psalm 137:4 "How shall we sing the Lord's song in a strange land."

Israel was in exile in Babylon, and their captors wanted them to sing the songs they sang back home. Israel was so discouraged and defeated that they didn't want to sing. They hung their musical instruments on the bushes and cried.

It makes me uncomfortable being a long way from home, even on a hunting trip. I enjoy myself since I know it is temporary, and it is a different experience, but it is always good to get back home to my wife and what I consider to be normal.

We are never really away from everyone we know. Jesus is with us no matter where we go. He says, "I am with you always, even to the end of the world."(Matthew 28:20) Are you away and feeling alone? Call on Him. He is as close as a prayer.

Prayer: Lord, thank You that I am never alone. In Jesus' Name, Amen.

AUGUST 29

When Life Begins

Psalm 139:13 "Thou hast covered me in my mother's womb."

The verse says that God recognizes life even before birth and provided a covering of protection. Human beings are "fearfully and wonderfully made," according to verse 14 of this same chapter. God has always known all about us, and we are very special to Him. We were born through the normal processes, but He created us.

Even wildlife management people protect the birth process. Hunting seasons are designed to protect quail, ducks, geese, etc., during periods of nesting and other wildlife when they are carrying their young. We may do it for selfish reasons like protecting our hunting, but we believe little ones should have a fair chance at survival.

Human babies should be protected even more. Thirty million babies have been aborted that weren't given a chance. Even ones that are almost full term are painfully killed and removed from the womb. We have more mercy for animals, at times, than we do for humans. God help us!

Prayer: Lord, help us to know that all life is precious in Your sight. Forgive us as a nation for killing babies and not giving them a chance. For Jesus' sake, Amen.

AUGUST 30

Hidden Evil

Psalm 139:24 "See if there be any wicked way in me, and lead me in the way everlasting."

What a tender and humble prayer! It admits that there may be evil in us that we don't know about. The intention is cleaning us up. Verse 23 says, "Know my heart." God would always hear and answer a prayer like that.

An albino deer is very easy to spot in the woods. He is white, and everything else is brown, green, and anything else but white. If it snowed in South Georgia he would be hard to see, but that hardly ever happens.

Some evil things we do are obvious because they are not socially acceptable. People frown on things like murder, stealing, and arson. They are like an albino deer in the woods, very obvious. More and more people disagree with God that certain things are evil. People are saying that some things may be right or wrong based on the situation, like sex outside of marriage or lying when the truth might be offensive or stealing if you are hungry. Sincere Christians will agree with God and the Bible and welcome these times when God reveals something we need to change.

Prayer: Lord, show me what I need to change and I will do it. In Jesus' Name, Amen.

AUGUST 31

In Prison

Psalm 142:7 "Bring my soul out of prison, that I may praise thy name."

I suppose that zoos are good for educating the public, and it is fine to have them. We would never see some animals if we didn't have them, but I would rather see them walking around in the wild.

There are people who, for the protection of others, have to be in prison. Some might be innocent, but most are not. It must be depressing to know that you will never be free again. If you are one of those, you can praise the Lord anyway and in a sense, be free.

Many walk around free or look that way, but they are in prison. They are bound by attitudes, habits, guilt, and sinful lifestyles. God does not accept their praise because they harbor known sin. No matter where we are, we can all be free. As Jesus was freed from the grave, He swung the bars open for us. We can confess and turn from our sin, ask Him in, and begin to give praise.

Prayer: Lord, I accept the freedom You give me by faith. Thank You for my freedom. Amen.

SEPTEMBER 1

He Knows My Name

Psalm 147:4 "He telleth the number of the stars; He calleth them by name."

Can you imagine that God knows all the names of the millions of stars of the universe and cared enough to name them? He created them and knows their name. Why would He care about how many there are, and why would He want to name them? It speaks of the love of God for His creation and His ability to know everything.

Have you ever tried to count a drove of wild turkeys running through the woods? They run ahead and drop behind, cross over one another, and raise and lower their heads. I really don't care so much about an accurate count. It isn't crucial. I just want to tell hunting buddies approximately how many I saw.

Jesus knows when a sparrow falls and knows the numbers of hairs on our head. He knows our names and everything else about all of us because

He loves and cares for us. How comforting it is that Creator God knows us that well and loves us anyway. Some of us were not loved by our parents and don't understand that kind of unselfish, giving love. Get used to it, and put your trust in the One who knows your name.

Prayer: Lord, what a humbling thought that You care so much for even me. I will try to believe that You do and give my life to You. In Jesus' Name, Amen.

SEPTEMBER 2

God Enjoys Us

Psalm 149:4 "The Lord taketh pleasure in His people."

What do you really enjoy about life? For many people, sports and recreation seem to be about it. That is all they talk about anyway–that last hunt, the next one, or the trophies on the wall. I'm afraid that is very self-centered and short-sighted.

God takes pleasure in His people. This psalm refers to people worshiping through dance and singing. God gets great pleasure in it. Saving the "meek," or those who humble themselves before Him, is a joy to Him.

We should get used to the idea that people, not things, matter to God. That is how it should be with us. Things are temporary, but people will live forever. We need to cultivate those permanent relationships with God and others.

Prayer: Lord, as Your Word says in Colossians 3:2, help me "set my affections on things above." In Jesus' Name, Amen.

SEPTEMBER 3

What Makes You Wise

Proverbs 1:5 "A wise man will hear and will increase learning."

I don't consider myself to be a great student of hunting, but I find myself listening to the advice of others about it. I even bought a video one time of turkey calls and how to use them. A serious hunter could spend most of his time learning, but he wouldn't be any wiser because true wisdom is about God.

Education is important. Some of us consider ourselves "educated" if we finish high school, and for sure if we finish tech school or college. We get a job and make a living, but if we stop there, we shortchange ourselves. We should continue to develop our minds by reading things other than the sports page and sporting magazines. I think it sharpens your mind and helps prevent you from becoming senile.

Still, education is incomplete without knowing God. That also should be a never-ending process. Education can be dangerous unless you have the love of Christ along with it. Knowledge can build an atomic bomb or generate electric power. One is for killing; the other is for giving life. Knowing God makes you truly wise.

Prayer: Lord, Solomon prayed for wisdom, and You granted it. Give me that wisdom to know You. For Christ's sake, Amen.

SEPTEMBER 4

Ignoring God's Counsel

Proverbs 1:25 "Ye have set at naught all my counsel, I will laugh at your calamity."

A man was caught hunting deer at night several years ago. The game warden took his gun and truck. I have no sympathy for him. Everybody knows it is illegal to hunt deer at night without a permit. Some thought the penalty was a little harsh, and maybe so. However, people who deliberately violate the law should have a stiff penalty.

Most of us are guilty of doing things we know are wrong and take our chances getting caught. We figure that the fun we have is worth more than the punishment we might get. Chances are, though, we might not even get caught.

With God, we always get caught if we disobey. I think the reason God laughs here is that it is so ridiculous to think He doesn't see or won't judge us. The sad thing is that we damage our relationship with Him and miss rewards in heaven. Always obey God. Don't cause yourself suffering.

Prayer: Lord, You are holy, righteous, all-seeing and just. Deliver us from ignoring Your counsel. In Jesus' Name, Amen.

SEPTEMBER 5

Thinking Like God

Proverbs 3:5 "Trust in the Lord with all thine heart and lean not unto thine own understanding."

As I have hunted over the years, I have learned that in order to be successful, you have to think like the animal you are hunting. You don't hunt squirrels in the open fields, but in the hardwoods. Rarely, if ever, do you find quail on the top of a hill. They are usually around the edge of grain fields near thick woods.

By the same token, to be successful in your work, you have to learn from the people who know your trade. You learn banking from bankers, computers from experts, and driving a truck from an instructor. I would never think of trying to be an air traffic controller just knowing what I know now.

God knows all about us, about the world He created, and about what lies ahead. I could go through life and make a mess of things very easily. Believing and trusting God is the best way to go. Learn to think like Him, and He will keep you on track.

Prayer: Lord, I am not as smart as I think. My conscience and my own thinking will fail me. Teach me Your ways through Your Word so that I can avoid the pitfalls of life. In Jesus' Name, Amen.

SEPTEMBER 6

The Loving Hand of Discipline

Proverbs 3:12 "Whom the Lord loveth, He correcteth."

Several men overloaded a small boat to cross a swift river to hunt wild hogs. Somehow, the nose of the boat plowed under the water, and one man went under. None of them had life jackets, and one couldn't swim and drowned. I don't know whether God's correcting hand was involved or not. I do know that the laws of nature and common sense were violated. God gives us free choices and sometimes we make fatal mistakes for which we cannot blame Him.

As we try to raise our children right, we have to correct them, and it hurts the child and parent. We must be careful to communicate love when we do discipline our children. We love them too much to just let them run wild. If we don't correct them, the law will have to in order to protect society.

If God just let everyone go his own way and allowed us to violate His law, it would destroy us all. That would not be love. We need discipline, and He loves us so much that He does it.

Prayer: Thank You, Lord, that You protect us from ourselves and each other by correcting us. Amen.

SEPTEMBER 7

God's Umbrella

Proverbs 6:20 "My son. Keep thy father's commandment, and forsake not the law of thy mother."

I built myself a deluxe deer stand with sides and a top that shields me from the rain. It surely is cozy when everybody else is getting soaked, and it keeps me hunting when deer are walking, while other hunters have headed for home.

Parents are a shelter for their children. God has given them wisdom over the years that can help children avoid trouble. It is their responsibility given by God. While children are still in the home, they should obey their parents and stay under their "umbrella." If parents lead them astray, they are accountable to God.

Children should feel secure and enjoy not having those responsibilities. It is simple. Just obey your parents. One day the children will have to make their own decisions.

Prayer: Lord, help us be worthy parents, and help our children to honor our instruction. For Your sake, Amen.

SEPTEMBER 8

Peacemakers

Proverbs 6:16–19 "Six things doth the Lord hate . . . he that soweth discord among brethren."

One hunter was telling another one about finding someone in one of his own deer stands. The second hunter responded, "Man, I wouldn't let him do that to me. I would give him a piece of my mind." That was not helpful and increased the bitterness. He could have down played it and helped to smooth over hard feelings.

Jesus said, "Blessed are the peacemakers," but some seem to try to increase tension to build a bond and loyalty for themselves. God hates it. We should be helping people build relationships rather than tearing them down. Try to make others look good and be a reconciler. It will bless you.

Prayer: Lord, we are often tempted to speak evil of others and join in criticizing someone. Help us to leave the judging to You. In Jesus' Name, Amen.

SEPTEMBER 9

Being Faithful

Proverbs 6:32 "Whosoever commiteth adultery with a woman lacketh understanding."

The Old Testament and New Testament, including the teaching of Jesus, have a great deal to say about adultery. Simply, that is having a sexual relationship with a person to whom you are not married, or when there is another living spouse. Saying it another way, when two people separate or divorce and then remarry or have sex outside of marriage, it is adultery and condemned as sin. This verse says it is stupid.

As men gather anywhere, including hunting trips, that kind of behavior can be encouraged or discouraged in conversations. Men often tell of their conquests, I suppose, to impress other men, but it is a shame and is nothing to be impressed about. Such talk does encourage men of weak character to do the same thing. Men who are strong in the faith find it repulsive and should let others know how they feel.

Be faithful to your spouse in thought and action. Don't divorce. Work things out or you both might soon be in adultery.

Prayer: God, give me strength to be faithful to my spouse and help us build a stronger marriage. For Your sake, Amen.

SEPTEMBER 10

Correction

Proverbs 9:8 "Reprove not a scorner."

Some dogs are "gun shy" and will leave the area when a gun is fired. Some can be trained not to do that. A good trainer removed that tendency from a dog for me once. Others will never be anything but pets. After a while, you realize you are wasting your breath trying to train them.

There are people like that who are so hard that they just ridicule and criticize instruction. They are know-it-alls and won't listen. The Bible says not to even try to correct them. They will only hate you and will damage your reputation. Let them alone until they show signs of change.

On the other hand, verse 9 in this same chapter says, "Instruct a wise man and he will be yet wiser." He will also "love you." Be a learner. Literally, anyone can learn something from anybody. Learn from correction, and accept it humbly.

Prayer: Give me a teachable spirit, Lord, so I can learn from correction. In Jesus' Name, Amen.

SEPTEMBER 11

Glad Fathers

Proverbs 10:1 "A wise son maketh a glad father."

Deer and their young, apparently, only relate together on a need basis. A fawn is weaned when he is old enough and may stay around the doe for a year or so for security. Then the buck is gone, and he and the fawn, according to my observations, have little or no contact.

Children and parents should be different from deer in this respect. They should enjoy one another's company even during the teen and young adult years, when so many times the children try to put distance between themselves and their parents. Children should be around their parents, learning all they can. Their peers aren't much help with wisdom. They are struggling, too. Parents should be approachable and tender with wise, sensitive counsel, not pushy and domineering,

Then sons and daughters have to make wise choices that bless the lives of every parent. They may do things differently, but it is always godly and sound. They also manage their finances wisely and are solid members of their church and community. What a joy!

Prayer: Lord, bless our children with wisdom and a true heart to serve You. That will make us glad. Thank You. Amen.

SEPTEMBER 12

Women with Brains

Proverbs 11:22 "As a jewel in a hog's nose, so is a fair women which is without discretion."

Have you ever noticed that does usually walk way ahead of a buck? I've always thought, "That is a stupid doe. She faces the danger first and the buck has the protective antlers." Probably that is the way the Lord protects a dominant buck, and though it looks dumb to me, it serves God's beautiful purpose.

Our verse says that a beautiful woman with no sense of right and wrong is like a precious jewel in a hog's nose. I've seen many a beautiful woman who becomes ugly when she opens her foul mouth, drinks alcohol, smokes, or lives an immoral life. The way a person looks, to me, often changes based on what I find their character to be.

By the same token, I have seen women who are really not very pretty, but when you get to know them, they become beautiful. "Beauty is only skin deep, but ugly goes to the bone" is only a partially true statement. Our verse for today is similar to the phrase from the movie "Forrest Gump"—"Pretty is, as pretty does." That kind of woman has brains!

Prayer: Lord, let me be like You—concerned about the outside and the heart. In Jesus' Name, Amen.

SEPTEMBER 13

Wealth that Lasts

Proverbs 13:11 "Wealth gotten by vanity shall be diminished, but he that gathereth by labor shall increase."

Several times, coaches have been hired by prestigious colleges who later found out that their resumes contained false information. The coaches were fired and had to take lower positions. Wild hog hunters created quite a stir in South Georgia when they claimed to have killed a one thousand pound hog. "National Geographic Magazine" dug up the buried bones and found it was a big hog, but not that big.

God says that people who get wealth in a dishonest way will lose it just as quickly. I have heard of people losing their entire inheritance gambling. Their forefathers might have gained it honestly, but vanity squandered it. That kind of violation of godly principles does not pay off in the long run, and more and more, very poor people deprive their families by playing the lottery and slot machines.

So many people reject the ideal of just plain hard work and try to get rich quick. You hear of people winning the lottery and being bankrupt in just a few years. Just work hard and save. You'll have enough. It is the godly thing to do.

Prayer: Lord, deliver me from "pipe dreaming" and give me honest work to support my family. In Jesus' Name, Amen.

SEPTEMBER 14

The Right Way

Proverbs 14:12 "There is a way which seemeth right to a man, but the end thereof are the ways of death."

When you are hunting coons, it is easy for them to confuse the dogs by "back-tracking," climbing from one tree to another, or crossing water. The dogs can be on the wrong trail, and the coon gets away.

The verse says that a person can think he is right and be dead wrong. We can be easily led astray; advertising does it sometimes. Ads are so crude at times, they can spark immoral thoughts. We can get head-over-heels in debt by wanting everything we see advertised.

We can be led astray spiritually, too. Unless we know the Bible and are close to God, we can go down the wrong trail in a heartbeat. Don't ruin your life. Do it God's way.

Prayer: Lord, let me know the right path and follow it, so that I will not fail You and my family. In Jesus' Name, Amen.

SEPTEMBER 15

Backsliding

Proverbs 14:14 "The backslider in heart shall be filled with his own ways."

My bird dog went to a trainer several years ago for about three months and came back doing a good job. I got busy working and didn't have time to hunt with him, so he lost ground. He just runs wild and flushes birds before I get there to shoot. He smells them, points, and then runs in on them. He is getting much better, thankfully.

Christians can become like that very easily. They might have joined a church, gone through confirmation, been baptized or sprinkled, and then lost interest. Maybe they attend church only on Christmas or Easter or just for weddings and funerals. They could even attend about every service, but their heart is just not in it. They have backslidden.

It is a miserable feeling to be that way. You don't feel right about it, and you'd like that to change. Well, just begin to tell the Lord about it, and ask Him to help. Begin reading your Bible every day. Tell your spouse about it, and ask her to pray for you. You'll see a change soon.

Prayer: Lord, I've backslidden. Draw me back to you, closer than ever. Thank You. Amen.

SEPTEMBER 16

Impulsiveness

Proverbs 14:15 "The simple believeth every word, but the prudent man looketh well to his going."

I have noticed mature deer walking through the woods. Every movement and suspicious noise or scent attracts their attention. They stop for long periods, move their ears around, and sniff the air. If they detect danger, they may just slip away, making little noise.

You have to be careful about who you believe. Wise people seem to have a sixth sense. Some know when advice is sound, but others act too soon in their personal lives, business dealings, and matters of morality. Impulsiveness can be destructive. A sudden, careless word, purchase, decision, etc., can be disastrous.

Christians who are close to God have an advantage. They have the Holy Spirit inside to guide them. My problem is that I sometimes struggle with what I want to do against what I know I should do. Simply do nothing rash until, after much prayer, you have that peace about what to do. Don't rush to judgment.

Prayer: I get myself in trouble sometimes when I act impulsively. Help me make godly decisions. In Jesus, Name, Amen.

SEPTEMBER 17

Anger

Proverbs 14:17 "He that is soon angry dealeth foolishly."

A man found skeletons of two large bucks in the woods that had locked antlers together, could not separate, and starved to death. They had gotten mad and fastened together. If they had known it would cost them their lives, they probably would have made a different decision. You see deer with broken antlers and scars on their bodies that probably came from fighting. They survived but are scarred for life.

Anger can be good if it is unselfish and not excessive. It can serve as a motivator to do good. Self control is a fruit of the Spirit, and when we have it, anger does not get out of control. Humans kill and injure each other because of anger. Anger usually comes because we feel someone has violated our rights. It is selfish.

Sometimes there is anger in families and no physical scars, but there are deep scars in the spirit. Words in anger cut deeply. Someone has said that words in anger are like bullets that have been fired. They can never be taken back. When you are angry, don't do or say anything. Wait until it passes, and spend some time in prayer.

Prayer: Lord, how I hate things I have said and done in anger. Forgive me and heal the wounds. In Jesus' Name, Amen.

SEPTEMBER 18

Loving Neighbors

Proverbs 14:21 "He that despiseth his neighbor sinneth."

Elk are territorial, I understand, and other wildlife, like bluebirds, as well. They become agitated when another animal gets too close.

Human beings are sometimes less than friendly to their neighbors as well. The Scripture today is not necessarily talking about treating them badly, but it could mean ignoring them. The next phrase in this chapter says, "He that hath mercy on the poor." The picture is of a person who failed to meet needs of a neighbor. He sins when he does that, but he does good when he shows mercy.

Today, we have become isolated and very selfish. In larger towns, we might not even know our next door neighbor. This is wrong. Jesus was outgoing and loved people. We have a great opportunity to show the love of Christ by showing interest in others and sharing our goods and faith with them.

Prayer: Lord, I confess I would rather be shut up in the house and watch a hunting show. Help me to be more outgoing and care more about people. For Jesus' sake, Amen.

SEPTEMBER 19

Truth

Proverbs 14:25 "A true witness delivereth souls: but a deceitful witness speaketh lies."

Hunters can tell some far-fetched tales. Really, I have learned to take some of them with a grain of salt. Though they rarely do any measuring or weighing, they give generous estimates and sometimes the estimate grows as time passes. If someone says the buck had a twenty inch spread, I register fifteen. If he estimates fifteen ducks, I register ten.

You might say, "Well, it is just hunting talk and stretching the truth a little doesn't hurt." My Grandma Lord used to say, "If a person will lie, he will steal." The Bible says truth matters. Truth saves souls, and lies hurt.

Whether you are just talking about hunting or something more important, it is better to just be quiet rather than lie. It hurts your credibility, and you will not be able to influence listeners to become Christians.

Prayer: Lord, help me to tell the truth, even if it makes me look bad. In Jesus' Name, Amen.

SEPTEMBER 20

Peace With Others

Proverbs 16:7 "When a man's ways please the Lord, he maketh even his enemies to be at peace with him."

I can see how that could be true. We know it is, because this is God's Word. Kindness, gentleness, self control, generosity, a loving attitude and other godly qualities surely would bring about peace, even with people who don't like us.

It is not very easy to act in godly ways, particularly among non-Christian hunters who might be very secular, use bad language, drink alcohol, and talk about their womanizing. That really irritates me, but that is when we really should be extra careful because of our testimony.

Put it into practice and test it out. Do you have a lot of disharmony with people? Your ways are not pleasing to the Lord. Examine attitudes and behavior to see which ones might not be pleasing to Him.

Prayer: I am at peace with some people. Show me what I need to change to be at peace with others. In Jesus' Name, Amen.

SEPTEMBER 21

Pride

Proverbs 16:18 "Pride goeth before destruction and a haughty spirit before a fall."

A hawk caught a rabbit in the middle of the highway and a log truck started coming. He opened his beak and lifted his wings in defiance. The truck kept coming and flattened him. He was so proud of that fresh kill that he was willing to take on the world. He made his point, but lost his life.

That happens to many people. Pride and ego destroy many relationships, including marriages. It is good to take pride in what you do, but it is different to have a "chip on your shoulder." Such people are defensive and never say, "I'm sorry," or admit they are wrong. They are stuck on themselves.

Prideful people don't feel that they need God. They brag that they are as good as anybody else and don't need any help. The opposite is humility. That is needed if we admit to God we have failed, and all of us have. He will forgive us and others will, too. We'll feel clean when we do.

Prayer: Teach me to be humble, Lord, like Jesus, and break down my unhealthy pride. In Jesus' Name, Amen.

SEPTEMBER 22

Respect for Older People

Proverbs 16:31 "The hoary (gray) head is a crown of glory."

Hunters look for that trophy turkey. You know you have him by the length of his beard and spurs. He gets that long beard by avoiding predators and sticking to a good diet. It is because of his "wisdom," if we can say that a turkey has wisdom.

The Bible says we should respect old people. Some Asian cultures, including Koreans, Chinese, and Japanese—at least some of them—even worship the elderly. That is idolatry, but the elderly should be treated with respect. They have been through the struggles of life and survived and have a great deal to offer.

Many young people treat older people with contempt, and they feel that they are out of date and irrelevant. Some old people harm themselves by letting themselves stagnate that way. The young person is trying to establish his own identity and often ignores or ridicules older people. We should value their wisdom and treat them with respect. Listen to them, and you can avoid some costly mistakes. The wisdom of older people and the energy and idealism of younger people can be blended together to honor God in the process.

Prayer: Thank You, Lord, for old, gray-headed people and what I can learn from them. Help me make them feel important and needed. For Your glory, Amen.

SEPTEMBER 23

Being Cheerful

Proverbs 17:22 "A merry heart doeth good like a medicine."

I declare, I believe there are times when my old bird dog is smiling. He may be just hassling, but he just looks happy when he is out running around. Let him go out and find birds then come back for that pat on the head. He runs in the yard chasing anything in his way and jumps up on people. It makes me feel good.

Cheerful people do me good, too, but hearing negative and depressing talk of others can get me down. I hate to see "phony" smiles, though. Some Christians argue all the way to church and then put a phony smile on to impress others and show how "holy" they are. That is hypocritical, and people see right through it.

We ought to be cheerful because it shows that we are at peace inside, and Christians, of all people, should be. When we turn our problems over to the Lord we can be cheerful, and then it is like a good medicine to us and others. Think of good and positive things. Have a sense of humor to break up tense and negative moments. Find humor in your problems. Others will feel better as well.

Prayer: I know it is just not Christian to be negative and complain or become depressed. Help me to surrender all of that to You and be cheerful. In Jesus' Name, Amen.

SEPTEMBER 24

Having Friends

Proverbs 18:24 "A man that hath friends must show himself friendly."

As many years as I have been going out into the woods, I have never seen even two bobcats together. They are always by themselves. When I do see one, it is usually chasing or stalking a squirrel or some other animal. They just aren't very friendly.

I have heard our children and others say, "That person has no friends. He is always by himself." Some of those "loners" get in trouble a lot and have a bad attitude. Many of the young people who have gone on shooting sprees in schools of late were loners. If you don't have friends, you are putting yourself at risk.

I would encourage you to develop some friends, and that is not easy if you are in the habit of having none. The Bible verse for today says for us to be friendly if we want friends. Go out of your way to speak to people. Ask them about their family and other things they are interested in. Don't talk much about yourself unless they ask, and then, be brief. Don't be confrontational in the beginning. Be around other people more.

Prayer: Help me to have friends so that I can have a positive influence on them and witness for Christ. In Jesus' Name, Amen.

SEPTEMBER 25

Laziness

Proverbs 19:15 "An idle soul shall suffer hunger."

Animals seem to always be looking for food. Rabbits can be seen many hours of the day and night eating. They seem to stir more in the cool of the day and at night and must constantly be on the move to survive.

I knew of an able-bodied sixty-year-old woman with grandchildren who was still depending on her eighty plus year old mother. The sixty-year-old also had to take care of a granddaughter because of a lazy daughter. It had become a family tradition to look to others for support. Other people rely on welfare when they could be working. My grandmother would have called them "dead beats."

People should be industrious and carry their own load. We should have a great deal of pride in accomplishing things and supporting our family.

Prayer: Lord, the Bible says that a person who does not work "should not eat." Help me to abide by Biblical principles and work. In Jesus' Name, Amen.

SEPTEMBER 26

Drinking

Proverbs 20:1 "Wine is a mocker, strong drink is raging."

Most hunting clubs do not allow alcoholic beverages on hunts. That is just good common sense, whether you are a Christian or not. You can't afford to get someone injured or killed because someone was drinking.

The second part of this verse says, "Whosoever is deceived thereby is not wise." It slows reflexes, dulls the mind, and impairs judgment. Drunk drivers kill thousands of innocent people every year. People steal, lie, abuse people, etc., when they are under the influence of alcohol. It doesn't make any sense to let drinking bring such pain to the family.

The main reason I don't drink, as I have previously stated, is the bad influence on others. We are accountable when we cause others to stumble. I would grieve myself to death if a grandchild followed my lead and became an alcoholic.

Prayer: Lord, I pray that You will make alcohol unattractive to people. May I never drink or do anything to lead someone astray. In Jesus' Name, Amen.

SEPTEMBER 27

Flattery

Proverbs 20:19 "Meddle not with him that flattereth with his lips."

I have heard that snakes "charm" their prey. It may be just talk, but some say that snakes look into the eyes of their prey, and the animal senses no danger and does not realize the snake is getting closer all of the time until it is too late.

Flattery is kind of like that. It deceitfully wins a person over by exaggeration or false praise. Men do it a lot to women they are dating. People have a tendency to do it to their boss or others in a position to do them favors.

Watch out for such people who "gush." They will deceive you if they can. Avoid flattering others. It will cause them to distrust you.

Prayer: Lord, teach me to watch for people who flatter so I won't be charmed and deceived. In Jesus' Name, Amen.

SEPTEMBER 28

What Pleases the Lord

Proverbs 21:3 "To do justice and judgment is more acceptable to the Lord than sacrifice."

The Lord would rather see us do the right thing than sacrifice an animal or do some heroic thing for Him. He does want us to sacrifice our time, talent, and resources in the name of Christ, but He would rather see us treat our fellow man in decent and honest ways. As a practical matter, we need both.

Fair and honest dealings with our hunting buddies (and others) are more important than tithing. Helping your friend dress his birds or clean his deer would be better than serving as an usher in the church. We only gain credibility as Christians when our faith gets outside the church walls. The love of Jesus in us does not exist unless it is expressed toward others.

We can't give or do enough to replace character. True worship is not so much giving our money as it is giving ourselves.

Prayer: Deliver us from the rituals of religion, and implant the love of Jesus in our hearts. In Jesus' Name, Amen.

SEPTEMBER 29

Mercy

Proverbs 21:13 "Whoso stoppeth his ears at the cry of the poor, he also shall cry himself and not be heard."

A red tailed hawk was apparently trying to catch a squirrel or rabbit along a fence behind our house and did not see the fence. When he made his dive, he wedged tight in the mesh and could not get out. A neighbor found him and he was still alive. A falconer from a local university drove out and removed him from the fence, but he had internal injuries and did not survive. The neighbor might have left the hawk in the fence to die, or the falconer might not have been interested in saving him, but they cared enough to try.

Though that was commendable, the Bible is talking about poor people and meeting their needs in the verse above, not helping animals in trouble. For one reason or another, some people are rich and others are poor. Poverty could mean laziness, but sometimes it doesn't. That issue is not addressed in the verse. It just says that if we don't help them when they ask us, we will someday be in need and not get the help we need.

We have no alternative about helping the poor. Sometimes we rationalize that people might "rip us off" or that they aren't worthy. Some even quote a Bible verse that says, "The poor will always be with us," and use that as an excuse not to help. I can't separate the truly needy from the "scam artists." We aren't judged by whether we gave to the right people or not but whether we helped those who asked. God will bless the intentions of our heart.

Prayer: Compassion is what You ask for, Lord. Deliver us from stinginess or hard-heartedness that might deprive others, but give us wisdom to give as You would. In Jesus' Name, Amen.

SEPTEMBER 30

Pleasure

Proverbs 21:17 "He that loveth pleasure shall be a poor man; he that loveth wine and oil shall not be rich."

There was a man in our little town who worked as little as possible and fished and hunted as much as possible. He and his wife had several children, and they barely got by. The children's teeth rotted out. His wife was industrious and kept them from going under. The man enjoyed pleasure and neglected his family. What a shame!

Most men I know work and support their families pretty well. In fact, sometimes both spouses work so that they can have many of the luxuries of life, but end up neglecting their marriage and children. On top of that, one or both of the parents feel like they need to spend all of their spare time in the woods hunting. Their family and church life suffers.

We need pleasure, but it can be abused. Don't let your family and your relationship to the Lord be compromised.

Prayer: Lord, help me to allow time first for You, then my spouse and children, and my job, and last of all, pleasure. In Jesus' Name, Amen.

OCTOBER 1

A Good Name

Proverbs 22:1 "A good name is rather to be chosen than great riches and loving favor rather than silver and gold."

It matters what other people think of you. What kind of reputation do you have? Being a "people pleaser" is not what I am talking about, but do people see you as an unselfish giver who lives for God and others or one who lives for himself?

When we hunt in South Georgia, we always have to be on the alert for rattlesnakes. There aren't that many, but if one bites you, it is usually "lights out." They have a bad name. You avoid them, wear snake boots, and are careful where you sit or step.

Your name or reputation is determined by what you say and do. You have to be careful. It is hard to overcome when you lose the confidence of those around you. Dishonesty, immoral activity, profanity, etc., taint our lives. People think you might sin again and say, "He can't be trusted." It may determine what job you might get, who might marry you, who will associate with you, and many other things.

Prayer: Lord, help me maintain a good name by following Your will. For Your sake, Amen.

OCTOBER 2

Spanking Children

Proverbs 23:14 "Thou shalt beat him with the rod and shalt deliver his soul from hell."

Heavy fines are put on hunters who violate the law. When I was a little boy, I was told the fine for killing robins was thirty dollars for each bird. Now in those days, that was a lot of money. I don't know whether the person who told me about the fine was telling the truth or not, but there must be strong deterrents for violating the law.

There is a raging controversy these days about how to discipline rebellious children. A psychologist forty years ago said not to spank them, and he has lots of followers even today to the point that children cannot be spanked in most public schools. Misbehavior there is out of control, and teachers are frustrated. Dr. James Dobson, a Christian psychologist, says to do it selectively and only for willful disobedience.

The Bible does not encourage abuse and no good parent would, I suppose, but it does allow for spanking. It is a good tool to have in reserve, but it should be used when everything else fails for rebellious children—not for accidents or hyperactivity. This must be an option to restore order to our homes and classrooms.

Prayer: Lord, may the discipline I use for my children be appropriate and without anger. In Jesus' Name, Amen.

OCTOBER 3

Calling Evil Good

Proverbs 24:24 "He that saith unto the wicked, 'Thou art righteous,' him shall the people curse, nations shall abhor him."

If a game warden began to ignore violations of game laws, things would soon be out of control. There would soon be no game to hunt or enjoy. If bad sportsmanship is accepted, then we are calling it good.

We are coming to the point where we are calling evil good. The Bible calls homosexuality evil, but we are on the verge of voting homosexual marriage into law. We are already striking down laws that regulate unwed cohabitation. It is against God's law. Gambling used to be illegal in most states, but now it is legal, and states promote the lottery.

Our unchanging God will never reduce His standards. If we want to please the Lord, we will go by God's Word, no matter what society accepts. We will be judged by His standards, not man's.

Prayer: O God, it breaks my heart to see where we are heading! Please turn us back to You. In Jesus' Name, Amen.

OCTOBER 4

Timely Words

Proverbs 25:11 "A word fitly spoken is like apples of gold in pictures of silver."

We hunters have a reputation for being "coarse" and even gross and insensitive at times. I think we like being labeled that way. We certainly wouldn't want to compliment anyone, because that would spoil our macho image. That is a part of the way we are, and we have a good time poking fun at each other and even putting each other down at times.

Words are so important, though. They are like gold framed in silver, the Bible says. Most of us have heard the phrase "silver tongued." That means saying the right thing at the right time to the right person. Men in the past, for example, would never curse in front of a woman. It was disrespectful. There is a time to be serious and use our words to build people up.

We can bring comfort, encouragement, harmony and a great deal of good (or evil) by what we say and how we say it. Tactful, kind, encouraging people are a blessing to all of us.

Prayer: Lord, help me to select words for the right moment. There are always people who need them. In Jesus' Name, Amen.

OCTOBER 5

Good for Evil

Proverbs 25:21 "If thine enemy is hungry give him bread to eat."

If you have ever noticed animals in the wild, the "rule of the jungle" is in effect. Natural enemies don't mix. Predators are on the attack, and the prey is trying to get away. This is one difference, among many, that distinguishes man from animals.

God commands people to be different from animals. They are to meet needs of even their enemies, rather than attack or even avoid them. This is because people are given the ability by God to love and forgive. Animals don't have that.

Some humans live by the law of the jungle, which pays evil for evil and sometimes evil for good. Christians have the power to do good for evil if they yield to God's will. God will give us the power if we have the will. That is "will power" to do good for evil.

Prayer: Lord, give me will power to live like You want humans to live. For Christ's sake, Amen.

OCTOBER 6

Choosing Workers

Proverbs 26:6 "He that sendeth a message by the hand of a fool cutteth off the feet."

During World War II, pigeons were used to carry secret messages that were crucial to the war. It was a tremendous idea and worked for a while, until the enemy learned about it and started shooting them down.

The warning given in Scripture is to be careful who you choose for important jobs, whether carrying messages or something else. Choose dependable people with Christian principles. We are only as effective as the people we have around us. A wise manager may not be the best one at everything but the one who surrounds himself with the best people.

The same goes for those who work in the church. Choose people who are committed to Christ and are called to serve. They might not be the most qualified or best trained, but if they have integrity and motivation, they will do well.

Prayer: Help me select people who know You and are committed to Your task of reaching our world. In Jesus' Name, Amen.

OCTOBER 7

Meddling

Proverbs 26:17 "He that passeth by and meddleth with strife belonging not to him is like one that taketh a dog by the ears."

I have never hunted wild hogs with dogs, but I am told that you ought not to bother one of those dogs when he is trying to catch a hog. In his excitement, he might even bite his master.

There have been cases of police officers being called to a home for domestic violence and getting shot themselves. That is their job, though it is very unfortunate. We have to learn to leave things alone that don't concern us. Overhearing and "butting in" to conversations is rude. Interfering in your neighbors' affairs is not welcomed. If violence or something illegal is occurring, call the police.

Parents sometimes are tempted to get involved uninvited in problems of their married children. A daughter or son might go to his parents with marital problems, and that is not wise. Couples should communicate in a civil way, work out their own problems, or see a Christian counselor for help.

Prayer: Lord, I am not here to solve everyone's problems. Give me wisdom to know how to minister in a Christian way when invited to help others. In Jesus' Name, Amen.

OCTOBER 8

Adding Fuel to the Fire

Proverbs 26:20 "Where no wood is, there the fire goeth out."

Near Aspen, Colorado, my tent mate during an elk hunt almost burned our tent down. He was starting a fire and thought it went out. He poured on more lighter fluid and there was a spark left, so it caught the can on fire. If we had not been at ten thousand feet where the air is thin, we would have been in a mess.

Our verse does mention fire, but the real subject is conflicts and arguments. If we are involved in such disputes, we should just let it die. You can add more "wood to the fire" and get it hotter. It is better to let things cool down and then work out differences in a rational way.

It takes two to make a conflict. The natural thing is to "carry your point," but that doesn't help and only makes things worse. Our competitive nature calls for winning the argument. When tempers flare, things are said that are never forgotten. Be a peacemaker. Don't add fuel to the fire.

Prayer: Lord, help me to swallow my pride when conflict comes and give You time to work out a peaceful solution. In Jesus' Name, Amen.

OCTOBER 9

Tomorrow

Proverbs 27:1 "Boast not thyself of tomorrow."

Imagine this. You buy your duck loads, select special equipment, and get an airline ticket to go to Arkansas to hunt. You get there, eat a good meal, joke around with the guys, and talk about the excitement of the next morning. You hang your clothes on the bed post and go to bed, really too excited to sleep. You finally do, but you don't wake up, for tomorrow never comes for you. What a chilling thought.

We are busy planning for the good things in this short life, but some of us do not make plans for life after death, which lasts forever. How short-sighted. Sooner or later, the hunts, ball games, and things we spend all of our time on will end, and a new life will begin. If we don't plan for that one, all is lost.

Enjoy yourself, but make plans for the *real* future, too. Commit your life to the Lord. That is your ticket. Arm yourself with the Word. Clothe yourself with the clothes of godliness. Hang around with other believers. Then, go in peace.

Prayer: Lord, please focus my attention on heaven rather than this temporary life. In Jesus' Name, Amen.

OCTOBER 10

Unexpressed Love

Proverbs 27:5 "Open rebuke is better than secret love."

An old bird dog can be lying in the pen half asleep, but you walk up, call his name, say a few encouraging words, give him a few pats on the head, and he will knock you down trying to get in the truck with you. That little affection really gets him going.

The Bible says it is better to chastise someone before their friends rather than love them and not tell them. You would never criticize your wife or your children in public, would you? That is a "no-no." However, God says that is better than not expressing your love for them. When confronted about not saying "I love you," you might erroneously say to your spouse, "If I didn't love you, I wouldn't have married you. If that changes, I will let you know." So many marriages of older people are dead because of that kind of attitude, and you never see them hug each other or touch affectionately. An older man kissed his sick wife, and she said, "That is the first time you have kissed me since I was in the hospital." That was at least a year before. Everyone in the room laughed, but I read her pain. Something had died.

Tell your spouse and children you love them often. Hug them and give them those warm smiles. Just reach over and touch their hand or cheek every now and then. You will see them perk up.

Prayer: Lord, how insensitive we are sometimes. Most of us are dying for affection. Help us to express love more openly and more often to our loved ones. Amen.

OCTOBER 11

Friends

Proverbs 27:17 "Iron sharpeneth iron; so a man sharpeneth the countenance of his friend."

Quail travel in coveys, except in the spring. They keep each other warm in the winter, serve as a warning system to each other concerning predators, and work together to find food. If they are scattered, you will soon hear them whistling and answering each other. They will soon be back together, because they need each other.

I made an angry statement as a naïve teenager—"I don't need anybody." That is false. Friends encourage each other by pats on the back and handshakes for a good job. They hold each other accountable if they see each other going astray. Everyone needs a close friend to talk to other than their spouse–someone of the same sex. Our best friend on earth should be our spouse, but we need close friends.

Sometimes there are things that no one else can understand, so our best friend should be Jesus. We can cry, confess our sins, and unload our burdens on Him. He is always there to comfort us.

Prayer: Lord, thank You for friends and, above all, that You want to be my best friend. Amen.

OCTOBER 12

Praise

Proverbs 27:21 "As the firing pot for silver and the furnace for gold; so is a man to his praise."

In a dove field one day, three doves flew by and through sheer luck and a little skill, I shot all three down. A nearby hunter shouted, "Did you kill all three? Dang!" That little bit of praise really charged me up.

Praise can be more than just encouragement. It can be like a refinery that removes impurities from gold and silver and makes them a higher quality metal. Praise encourages more of the same.

Praise can purify if we only praise what is pure, like good behavior. An approving smile with a nod of the head, words of praise, or a pat on the back reinforces good or bad behavior. If we laugh at dirty jokes or remarks that belittle others, we will get more. That is one way God purifies us. We get His approval when we do right and feel guilty when we do wrong.

Prayer: Lord, may I encourage good in others by what I praise. In Jesus' Name, Amen.

OCTOBER 13

Being Jumpy

Proverbs 28:1 "The wicked flee when no one pursueth, but the righteous are bold as a lion."

Deer can be walking through the woods nibbling and suddenly snort, raise their flags, and vanish into the trees. Actually, they were probably spooked by a smell or something they saw, but it appears they did it for no reason. It is a matter of survival, so they are very cautious.

A war veteran who had just returned from Vietnam many years ago told me he couldn't sleep at night and found himself flinching at loud noises during the middle of the night. Memories of avoiding the enemy and being under attack flashed back into his mind. I hate that he has to go through that.

Our verse talks about wicked people running when no one is after them. That is a guilty conscience. People who have done something wrong live in fear that law enforcement will catch them. People unfaithful to their spouses fear getting caught. That must be a miserable feeling to walk around every day filled with guilt and fear. We don't have to be "jumpy," for we can "come clean" and make things right with God and others.

Prayer: If we are forgiven and right with You and others, we don't have to be jumpy. Give me a clear conscience. In Jesus' Name, Amen.

OCTOBER 14

Value of Foresight

Proverbs 29:18 "Where there is no vision the people perish."

Many deer are killed by cars on the highways every year. I wonder how that happens, since they are usually so alert. You would think they would look ahead enough to say, "You know, I'd better stay here on the side of the road until that car passes by." They must not be able to judge speeds and distances very well.

Some people have a problem looking ahead and making good decisions that help them prosper or avoid danger or make moral judgments. Other people follow them and "perish" or are led astray. They are following someone with "no vision," as the Bible calls it.

With vision, a person can see the signs and make adjustments. Spiritual vision sees the value of walking close to God and leading family and others in that direction.

Prayer: Lord, help me to be a person of vision who can see far enough to lead people to You. In Jesus' Name, Amen.

OCTOBER 15

Temper

Proverbs 29:22 "A angry man stirreth up strife."

Squirrels seem to get upset at the drop of a hat. If something gets too close, they begin to chatter and fluff their tail. I don't know whether they are scared, mad, or just warning the un-welcomed guest.

I have seen many people like that. If they don't get their way or somebody does something they don't like, they get furious and throw a tantrum. We call them "rotten" and it is usually because their parents let them get their way by throwing tantrums. Those parents can be heard saying, "Don't do anything to make him upset," and they tiptoe around him to please him the best they can. They have raised a very selfish child. He will cause turmoil everywhere he goes.

This type of person can't get along with people because they keep getting in his way. He lives for himself, which is just the opposite of Jesus, who gave His life for others. Christ can become Lord of a life like that and change it completely.

Prayer: Lord, help me give You control, so that I stay in control of my temper. In Jesus' Name, Amen.

OCTOBER 16

Badmouthing

Proverbs 30:10 "Accuse not a servant unto his master, lest he curse thee and thou be found guilty."

If you want to get on the bad side of a hunter quickly, say bad things about his coon dog or bird dog. He will write you off in a heartbeat. His dog is kind of a part of him, and he takes it personally, like a Georgia Bulldog fan when you talk about his "dogs."

The most cowardly thing I know is saying bad things behind someone's back, whether they be true or not. Whether we mean to damage people or not, we do. When we criticize an employee to an employer, we could destroy his career. If you say something bad about someone's mate, it could cause them problems. Why would we intentionally say bad things about people? Maybe we are angry with them or expect to be elevated in the eyes of listeners, but it does just the opposite. Be careful what you say.

The Bible says in Ephesians 4:32, "Be ye kind one to another, tenderhearted, forgiving one another." The Christian way is to say kind things about others. If you must point out a fault, do it to the person involved in private and in a gracious way.

Prayer: "Badmouthing" is a sin, we know. Help us, Lord, to pray for others rather than participate in badmouthing them. In Jesus' Name, Amen.

OCTOBER 17

Misquoting God

Proverbs 30:5–6 "Every word of God is pure, add thou not unto His words, lest He will reprove thee and thou be found a liar."

In hunting magazines, you can find ads for all kinds of hunting dogs, such as treeing dogs and bird dogs. They offer pedigrees and papers, but I wouldn't buy one unless I could try him on a hunt. Dogs with good blood lines can be "bummers," too. They need to be tested.

God's Word does not need to be tested, for He always speaks the truth. The Bible is not open to debate, though there is plenty of debate about it. We just need to apply it to our lives and live by it.

Some groups add other books and call them "God's Word," but our verse says that He will reprove you and you will be found a liar. Some claim to be able to add to what Jesus said as truth even today. Anyone doing that is claiming to be God, and there is but one God. The Book of Revelation in the Bible says that the curses of that book will be brought upon anyone who adds or subtracts from it. (Revelation 22:18–19)

Prayer: Lord, as You have commanded us, I will stick by Your Word, the Bible. Give me wisdom to live by it. In Jesus' Name, Amen.

OCTOBER 18

Handling Success

Proverbs 30:21–22 "The earth is disquieted . . . for a servant when he reigneth."

I wonder how a buck responds to the herd and the rest of the bucks when he finally becomes the dominant buck. Does he attack them and make them conform? I suppose few people know.

The Bible says it is disastrous when a slave becomes king. He just doesn't know how to handle himself and abuses the privilege. You have seen it, and I have, too, when a person gets lots of money or moves up quickly in an organization. Too many times, it turns sour. The most successful people I know have good relationships with others and manage their business wisely when they get to the top.

Some people develop a "holier than thou" attitude when they become Christians. Others sense it and are turned off. We need to remember that Christians are not "better" than anyone else. We are just saved and have nothing to brag about.

Prayer: Lord, help me to be humble enough to handle success. In Jesus' Name, Amen.

OCTOBER 19

Praising Your Wife

Proverbs 31:28 "Her children rise up and call her blessed; her husband, also and he praiseth her."

I have noticed nothing among animals, like what God expects of a husband for a wife, and vice versa. Animals act on instinct, their senses, and what is happening around them to protect their own well-being. Turkeys strut around a lot and show themselves off, but no animal I know of gives praise to any other. God expects more of human beings.

People can be as insensitive as animals sometimes, only meeting their own personal needs. Even animals need positive reinforcement, I believe, but wives and children need praise, as do husbands. Most of our wives never get much of that. They cook and clean, work another job, and take care of the children. That is a heavy responsibility. They get worn out and discouraged at times but go on anyway.

Let them know you appreciate what they do. Give them a break and let them go to the mall without the kids, take them out to eat, and compliment them for a good job. Don't criticize. Hug them often (even when you don't want sex), smile at them a lot, and court them like you did when you were dating. Don't take them for granted.

Prayer: Lord, my spouse is so special to me. Help me to look for the good points and praise her and be sensitive to her needs. For Your kingdom's sake, Amen.

OCTOBER 20

Discouragement

Ecclesiastes 1:3 "What profit hath a man of all his labour which he taketh under the sun."

We plant food plots every year in several places. One year, we planted a very large one in a damp bottom. We harrowed it up, fertilized, and planted some very expensive seed. It began to rain and rain. It filled ankle deep with water and stayed that way all winter. All that work was down the drain.

The preacher in Ecclesiastes saw the same old thing day after day and became depressed. It all seemed to be futile and meaningless. The aggravations and troubles had gotten to him, even though he was a preacher and should have known better.

All of us have those times when we wished we could stay in bed. One thing after the other goes wrong. The preacher came to his senses later and had a change of heart. Are you down? Find a quiet place and tell the Lord about it. He always hears. Sleep on it. Things will look better in the morning. Don't make any sudden decisions when you are depressed or discouraged.

Prayer: Lord, I am down and feel that way often. Help me to get Your perspective. All is well. Thank You. Amen.

OCTOBER 21

Emptiness of Things

Ecclesiastes 2:10–11 "Whatsoever mine eyes desired, I kept not from them . . . and all was vanity and vexation of spirit."

How many cows does a bull elk need? I was waiting for elk to cross a ridge after I had heard a shot not too far away. I learned later that our group had killed the bull. Then I saw cows coming and I lay down in the snow. I counted fifty-two as they passed about two hundred yards from me. Did all of those cows belong to one bull? He was dead and had nothing to show for it.

Our verse says the writer didn't deny himself anything. Other verses say he bought houses, tried pleasure, and became very wealthy, but nothing satisfied him. He tried wine, women, and song as well. How much does a person have to have before he is happy? The answer is simple. *Things won't ever make you happy!*

I've tried that and it didn't work for me, either. I only found peace by living for the Lord. There is nothing wrong with "things" unless you put them ahead of God. Focus on serving Him and others. Get your mind off getting things to make yourself happy.

Is this your prayer?: I've got guns, hunting buddies, dogs, and everything a person really needs, but I am still not at peace. Help me turn my attention from things to You. In Jesus' Name, Amen.

OCTOBER 22

Seasons

Ecclesiastes 3:1 "To everything there is a season."

In late winter or early spring, deer shed their antlers. Does give birth in the summer. The rut comes in the fall and the cycle begins all over again. Things are born, mature, reproduce, get old, and die.

There is a time to weep, and a time to laugh, a time to morn and a time to dance. There is no end to the list of things that happen in a person's lifetime. Some deal well with them and take them in stride, and others don't. How can you be ready for the ups and downs of life?

Keep things in balance by trusting in God. He can prepare us for anything, and there is nothing he can't bring us through. Plan for the unexpected, but turn your worries over to God. Save some money, allow extra time, be patient, enjoy people, and don't take things too seriously.

Prayer: Lord, You are in charge. I will prepare and do all I can, but I will be satisfied with what the seasons of life bring. You do all things well. Thank You. Amen.

OCTOBER 23

Purpose of Worship

Ecclesiastes 5:1 "Keep thy foot when thou goest to the house of God, and be more ready to hear than to give the sacrifice of fools."

Doves gather in the fields in the morning, and at times, late in the afternoon. It's hard to predict when they will be there, but if there is grain, they will be there. The reason they show up is because they are hungry. It is not a social call to have fellowship with the other doves.

People go to church for many reasons, and I'm not sure it is always for the right reasons. Why do they go at Christmas and Easter when they don't go any other time? I'm glad they go then, at least. Whether we are in that group or attend every Sunday, we may go there to meet our hunting buddies, show off our finery, or do like some politicians and go there to get votes. God knows their hearts.

If we go for the wrong reasons, that is a "sacrifice of fools." The Bible says we should go to hear with the intention of worshiping and obeying God. Do you go for any other reason?

Prayer: Lord, I want to worship You, so turn my thoughts away from anything else. In Jesus' Name, Amen.

OCTOBER 24

Making Promises

Ecclesiastes 5:5 "Better is it that thou shouldest not vow than that thou shouldest vow and not pay."

One day I was talking to a man after church and he said, "I know you like to hunt. I'm going to invite you to a dove shoot next season." The season came and went, and it never happened. He could have just forgotten, but I learned that he decided to rent his fields to other hunters. That is fine, but he should have never made the promise, or when things changed, he should have called and let me know. His integrity is in question, for sure.

We make promises, as that man did, by borrowing money, getting married, having children, joining the church, and many other ways. All of these things obligate us to people and to God. When we shirk our responsibilities, God and others are violated. Our reputation is at stake.

Some people say, "I don't make promises because I don't want to break them." Those types just don't want to commit, because they know that if something else comes along, they don't have the backbone to stick to it. It is far better to be servant enough to commit and have integrity enough to follow through.

Prayer: Lord, make me willing to make and follow through on my commitments. In Jesus' Name, Amen.

OCTOBER 25

Inheritance

Ecclesiastes 7:11 "Wisdom is good with an inheritance."

My dad died a few years ago and left us a small piece of land, which is ideal for hunting. If we had managed things differently, we would probably not have the place to hunt.

So many inherit land, money, and other things, and all of it is soon gone. They have nothing to show for it because they are "consumers" rather than builders, like their forefathers. I have heard of professional athletes who made millions in salaries and ended up broke.

It is very wise, according to the Bible, to manage your inheritance well. New cars, boats, jet skis, four wheelers, and such are fun for a while, but they are depreciating assets. Spend some excess money on things that increase in value. Save some money out of every paycheck. Tithe to your church. That type of mentality will build an inheritance.

Are you thinking about leaving an inheritance to your wife and children? That is a good idea, but don't leave too much so that they don't have to work if they are able. That will destroy their initiative. Leave some money to a church or missions organization, so you can still serve the Lord after you die.

Prayer: Thank You, Lord, for Your gift to me through my parents. Lead me to be a good steward of it for Your glory. Amen.

OCTOBER 26

Risk

*Ecclesiastes 11:1 "Cast thy bread upon the waters:
for thou shalt find it after many days."*

Quail have a dilemma when they are pointed by a bird dog and the hunter is standing close. They can sit still and be caught by the dog or shot on the ground by the hunter—a sure death—or they can fly and have some chance of getting away. They fly, and most of them do escape.

It is risky to "cast your bread upon the waters." You might never get it back and be hungry. A person must learn to take some calculated risks. Weigh the advantages and disadvantages and make a decision. You run the risk of failing, but you fail for sure if you do nothing. Big successes are built on many small failures from which we have learned.

Faith in Christ is "casting your bread upon the waters," also. There is a chance you might be wrong. We don't know all of the answers to our questions about God or the Bible. I would rather make a decision to live for Christ, which is a good life anyway, than take an even bigger risk of going to hell.

Prayer: Lord, may I never be afraid to step out in faith and risk, particularly on my faith. In Jesus' Name, Amen.

OCTOBER 27

Youth Well Spent

Ecclesiastes 12:1 "Remember now thy Creator in the days of thy youth."

Young people, as a whole, want to spend time doing "fun things." Even their parents fall into the trap of encouraging their children to involve themselves in hunting and other sports and neglect things that are far more important. Many of them would say that it is important family time, and I couldn't agree more. Get out in the woods with the kids and enjoy one another. You won't regret spending time with them.

Why not spend time with them doing something of eternal value, like going to church? We make great sportsmen and poor churchmen out of them far too many times. They will value what you value. Kids really don't care how you spend time with them, as long as you do.

If they see you spend time serving the Lord, they are likely to do the same. If you spend most of your time on the deer stand or duck blind, they will think that is the most important thing. Don't teach them to waste their young years on things that won't matter. Teach them to give the strength of their youth serving the Lord.

Prayer: Help me to use my young years for You and to teach my children to do the same. For Your sake, Amen.

OCTOBER 28

Old Man's Conclusion

Ecclesiastes 12:13 "Fear God and keep His commandments for this is the whole duty of man."

The big bucks aren't easy to get. It seems they disappear after they get to eight pointers. By the time they get that old, they learn how to avoid danger pretty well. I don't suppose an old twelve pointer sits them down and says, "Well, boys, it's dangerous out there. Let me tell you how I made it this far."

Fortunately for us, we have the advantage of the experiences of the writer of Ecclesiastes, who went through it all. His advice is, "Fear God." The next phrase says, "For God shall bring every work into judgment." He had tried life both ways—with and without God.

He is right. We avoid dangers of this life if we would just follow his advice and "fear God."

Prayer: Lord, I don't want to make the mistakes of others. Help me learn and live. In Jesus' Name, Amen.

OCTOBER 29

Rebellion

Isaiah 1:2 "I have nourished and brought up children, and they have rebelled against me."

Eagles, we are told, have to push their little ones out of the nest to get them started. Fawns have to have strong encouragement by their mothers to stop nursing. It is normal for little ones to finally leave the nest and be "weaned." Eventually, they must be self-sufficient.

Human mothers, at least most of them, would like for their children never to leave home. Some children would like it, too, and some continue to "sponge" off their parents long after they should be on their own. Extreme cases involve children who have retarded development physically, emotionally, or spiritually. Healthy children remaining at home after they become adults is usually an unhealthy thing. Another extreme is rebellion, where children reject the leadership of parents too early and either leave or become hostile in the home.

God wants us to depend more and more on Him, but we rebel. He has given us life, provided for all of our needs, and blessed most of us with good health. Many of us were born in a free country. We forget that we belong to God and reject His leadership, even though He made it all possible.

Prayer: Lord, You made me and I will follow and obey You. Help me, please. Thank You. Amen.

OCTOBER 30

Unclean

Isaiah 6:5 "Then said I, woe is me for I am undone, because I am a man of unclean lips."

I guess deer hunting is the dirtiest sport there is. By the time you put "doe scent" on you, drag a buck hundreds of yards through the mud, load him in the truck, skin him, cut him up, and bury the remains, you are sweaty, bloody, and stink to high heaven. Your wife won't let you in the house.

Spiritually, we get that way to God. Our "white lies," lustful thoughts, bitterness toward others, selfishness, prejudices, etc., make us stink before holy God. We have a bad memory, though, and think we are "squeaky clean."

Isaiah the prophet came to realize what we all should. We are unclean. When we can confess that and commit to change, God will forgive us and cleanse us. Man, a good warm shower and soap feel good after a hunt! It's even better to know God can cleanse our soul.

Prayer: I offer myself to You, Lord. Make me clean and pure. In Jesus' Name, Amen.

OCTOBER 31

I Will Go

Isaiah 6:8 "Whom shall I send and who will go for us? Then said I, 'Here am I, send me.'"

Quail hunting is probably my favorite sport. You put that old dog out and don't have to say anything. He is jumping fences and crisscrossing the field. Soon, if you are lucky, he is frozen like a picture on what you sent him for.

We are kind of like God's bird dog. Just as we send our dog to point birds, God has sent us to find people who are hungry spiritually and tell them about the Lord. To see the old dog point, the birds get up, and to knock one or two down is a great thrill. The most satisfying feeling in the world, though, is telling someone about Jesus and hearing him commit his life to Christ.

Some of us are commanded to leave our own land and go somewhere to spend our lives telling others about Jesus. Are you obeying His call?

Prayer: Lord, I am listening and hope I will always be obedient to Your call. Make me willing, if I am not already. In Jesus' Name, Amen.

NOVEMBER 1

A Child Is Given

Isaiah 9:6 "Unto us a child is born. Unto us a son is given."

The cutest things in the world to me are newborn or newly hatched wildlife. A tiny fawn with his spots and wobbly legs, little quail about the size of your thumb, baby ducks paddling trying to keep up with their mother, or baby possums hanging onto their mother are all unforgettable sights.

Human babies are cute, too, but the baby mentioned in this verse was not like other babies. Yes, he was a normal baby born of a woman like everyone else, but He had no earthly father. He was the virgin-born Son of God who would be called "wonderful, counselor, the mighty God, the everlasting Father, the Prince of Peace."

His name is Jesus. He was born, lived thirty-three years, was crucified, and raised from the tomb. People who believe in Him are His children and will live with Him forever.

Prayer: I believe in the Christ child and give my life to Him. Thank You for saving me. Amen.

NOVEMBER 2

True Measurement

Isaiah 11:4 "With righteousness shall He judge the poor."

There is a Boone and Crockett standard of measurement to judge antler size that determines whose animal is the largest and most symmetrical of all those taken with a gun. It is very strict and precisely measured to make sure it is accurate. A great deal is riding on it.

Over three hundred Old Testament verses refer to Jesus, the perfect, righteous judge. Human measurements and standards are prone to error and are really meaningless, anyway, in the long run. In eternity, there will be no recognition or reward for Boone and Crockett record bucks and no "big buck" contest.

The judgment of Jesus is the only one that will matter, and that will not be done by a tape measure, but by records God keeps in the "Book of Life." Rewards will be based on the life we have lived.

Prayer: Lord, put my mind on the way all of us will be judged. In Jesus' Name, Amen.

NOVEMBER 3

Seek and Read

Isaiah 34:16 "Seek ye out of the book of the Lord and read."

My impression is that sportsmen don't read much other than sporting magazines, if that. Sometimes, I think we only look at the pictures. My wife teases me that the first thing I go to in the paper is the sports page. She is right. I do read a lot of books, though.

We need to read some stuff like biographies of good presidents, famous preachers, and others we can learn from. I like history, particularly about World War II and the Civil War.

Most important of all, we should be reading the Bible every day. Find a good translation, like the New American Standard, and start with the book of John in the New Testament and read one chapter a day. It will bless you, and you will be changed.

Prayer: Lord, teach me to stretch my mind by reading good books and the Bible. In Jesus' Name, Amen.

NOVEMBER 4

Fear

Isaiah 35:4 "Say to them of a fearful heart, be strong, fear not, behold your God will come with vengeance."

Wildlife of all kinds have to be on their toes all of the time because of the real dangers they face. Their senses are tuned to pick up any hint of a predator. Their survival depends on it.

We need to be cautious and not reckless. Driving too fast, leaving loaded guns lying around, and ignoring dangers of ticks, snakes, and other creatures in the wild is not wise. There is a difference between careful and being fearful.

Being careful is protecting yourself and others from real dangers. Fearfulness is excessive caution about real dangers and paranoia about things that hardly ever happen or things that are uncomfortable. We have to avoid recklessness and trust God with the rest. Living in constant fear is a type of slavery. Nothing touches Christians unless God gives the okay, and we should never fear what He wants to happen to us.

Prayer: Lord, help me to know that I have nothing to fear because You are my protector. In Jesus' Name, Amen.

NOVEMBER 5

Trust

Isaiah 36:4 "What confidence is this wherein thou trustest?"

The servant of the enemy of Israel asked this question of Hezekiah, the king of Israel, essentially saying, "You can't trust your God or another nation to defend you." He was trying to get Israel to give up hope and surrender.

Usually, wild animals have one or more in their group watching for danger. They trust him or her to warn them. Families need a trust relationship. Can your spouse trust you to be faithful, to provide for the needs of the family, and to tell the truth? I couldn't marry someone I couldn't trust.

We know that people will sometimes let us down, and they just cannot provide all that we need. Neither money, power, nor anything else can be trusted to meet the needs of the human heart. God can. In life and in death, He can provide peace, security, comfort, and salvation. Put your trust in Him.

Prayer: Lord, I will not put my trust in anything or anyone but You. For Jesus' sake, Amen.

NOVEMBER 6

Forever

Isaiah 40:8 "The grass withereth, the flower fadeth, but the word of our God shall stand forever."

Just about everything is temporary. Boone and Crockett records are broken every year, a brand new gun gets old and scratched, and the old bird dog gets old and dies. The newness of things wears off. I'm not as excited about new things as I used to be. People are born, grow old, and die. I'm not being morbid; that is just the truth. People shouldn't get all depressed about it, but they should keep it in mind.

The Bible teaches that some things are forever. One thing is God's truth, the Word. Man's opinions change with time. Scientists are revisiting their opinions regularly. They used to believe the world was flat, and doctors used to bleed people to get rid of their diseases.

Another thing that is permanent is the soul of man. We can be with God forever or separated from Him forever. I choose to be with Him, don't you?

Prayer: Lord, I believe Your Word will stand forever. Help me to live it. In Jesus' Name, Amen.

NOVEMBER 7

Strength

Isaiah 40:31 "They that wait upon the Lord shall renew their strength."

The strength in the bodies of wild animals is amazing. A black snake or king snake can crush a rattlesnake and burst the skin. A deer can jump high fences. A squirrel can literally run from the ground to the top of a tree without stopping. Most men I know struggle to pull their body high enough to do one chin-up.

Spiritual motivation and the power to live a victorious life doesn't come from wanting it to happen or working ourselves up to it or taking some drug to get us going. It doesn't come from transcendental meditation or some other "trick" that we might think of. It isn't "mind over matter," either, or "making things happen."

"Waiting upon the Lord" means preparing through prayer and Bible study, listening for His will, and moving on it. We act hastily and in our own strength without hearing from God; and what He does not call us to do, He does not bless. We wear ourselves out for nothing. It doesn't mean we should be lazy. He tells us what to do and energizes His servants with power and endurance beyond themselves.

Prayer: Lord, You say that Your yoke is easy and Your burden is light. Thank You for the power You give to live an obedient life. Amen.

NOVEMBER 8

Silence

Isaiah 41:1 "Keep silence before me and let the people renew their strength."

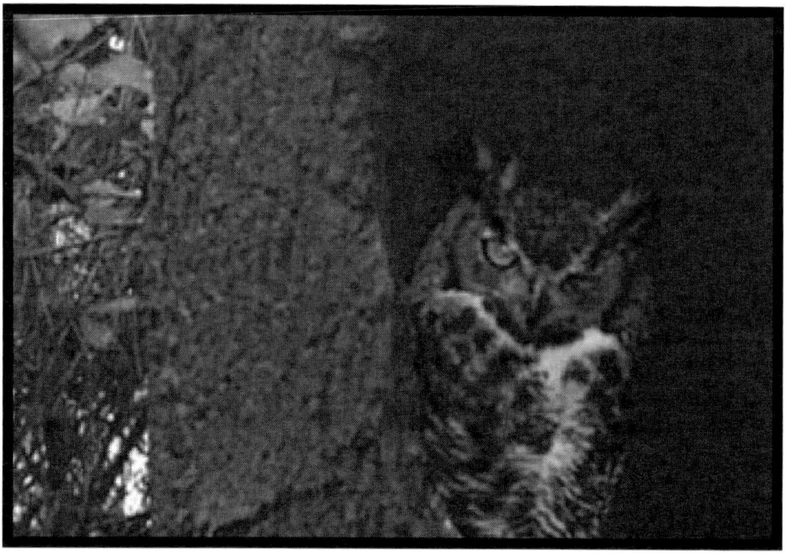

Being in the woods after dark on a dark night should be experienced by everyone. All you hear, in our part of the country, is an occasional whippoorwill or the blood-curdling hoot of a great horned owl. Nocturnal creatures move quietly searching for food, and the others are nestled in their hideouts being refreshed. All of them find places sometime during the day or night for silence. Their survival depends on it.

Many people these days are tired, irritable, and try to make it with clouded minds. We rush around from one activity to another to entertain ourselves, or we run from one job to another to pay the bills for things that don't make us happy. We allow small children's hyperactivity to keep us running all hours of the day and night until we are exhausted and have no time or energy to really communicate. Road rage, where people shoot one another for getting in the way, is a reflection of what many are feeling.

Be silent! Give God time to catch up with you. Teach the children to be still and talk. Families need time to sit and listen to each other without the TV, radio, or other noise on. Have at least one quiet meal together every day. Read quietly to the children. Pray. God will break through and we will find rest and our lives can be under control.

Prayer: Lord, I've got too much going on. I can't hear You speak because I can't hear myself think. Help me to be silent before You. In Jesus' Name, Amen.

NOVEMBER 9

Encouragement

Isaiah 41:6 "And everyone said to his brother, be of good courage."

As wild turkeys forage through the woods, you will hear a "yelp, yelp, yelp." A woodpecker will hammer and sing his song. Sparrows dart about and do their little "di, di, dit." If you listen closely, you can hear a grunt or bleat from a deer.

They don't do all of that for themselves. They are encouraging one another. It is comforting to know you're not by yourself. A bob white quail will whistle, and another will answer, and then it is quiet. They found each other.

We need to encourage one another. Men don't like to be mushy, but they like to hear, "Hey, that was great," or get a call from a friend out of the blue, or have a consoling pat on the shoulder. A good-natured verbal jab or friendly handshake makes all the difference in the world. It demands that we quit thinking about ourselves and think of encouraging others.

Prayer: Lord, help me think about how I can build others up who might be hurting very badly today. In Jesus' Name, Amen.

NOVEMBER 10

Light

Isaiah 42:6 "And give thee . . . for a light to the Gentiles."

As a hunter travels to his stand well before daylight, he uses as little light as possible. In unfamiliar territory and trying to find a well hidden stand off the beaten path on a very dark night, you have to have some light. You don't want to spook the deer that might be bedded down near the stand, yet you don't want to get lost or step on a snake.

Isaiah, seven hundred years before it happened, prophesied about a Savior, Jesus Christ, who came as a "light." Like a flashlight gives light for the next step, Jesus came showing mankind the way to go. I am told that some animals are drawn to the light of a fire, maybe out of curiosity because it is strange. Some people were drawn to Jesus and found that he was light. Some were "spooked" because they loved darkness.

Jesus said that we "are the light of the world." (Matthew 5:14) He also said not to put our light under a basket, but let it shine. As the light o Jesus shines through us, people will be attracted, and if they see that we ar "real," many will put their trust in Jesus.

Prayer: Lord, let my light shine brightly for You. In Jesus' Name, Amen.

NOVEMBER 11

Forgetting

Isaiah 43:18 "Remember ye not the former things."

At the beginning of deer season, deer seem to be plentiful. I would imagine that most of the ones taken are taken on opening day. The further you go into the season, the fewer you see. You see tracks, but no deer. Their memory of scents, sounds, and human beings walking around causes them to change their patterns.

Memory is sweet and helpful at times, but God told His people to forget some things—the bad things of the past. He said, "I will do a new thing." They could forget their troubles and idolatry.

There are some things that people need to forget. Ungodly memories, dirty jokes, and filthy language should be forgotten. Un-thoughtful or unkind words should be as well. We should be less sensitive to criticism. Forget those bad things you did that keep popping up and causing you pain. Damaging things others have done to you should be erased. All of these can make you a slave. Put it all behind you. Forgive yourself and others and be free.

Prayer: Lord, thank You for the beautiful memories I will treasure forever, but deliver me from those that enslave me. In Jesus' Name, Amen.

NOVEMBER 12

Idol Worship

Isaiah 44:17 "And the residue thereof he maketh a god."

The prophet describes how people take a tree that God planted, nourished, and grew, and used parts for their comfort. Then they take what is left, carve a god to worship, and forget the God who made it. We might say, "How foolish to worship a piece of wood!" How true that is.

It is like a gobbler that sees a hen decoy and hears the enticing yelps of the hunter's box call. It all looks and sounds good. He learns too late that he had been watching and listening to the wrong things.

So many of us are so busy climbing the ladder of success that we don't realize the ladder is leaning against a rotten wall. Is what you are counting on going to give you what you want in the end? Will a nice house, money, or a nice truck really satisfy you? Nothing will count in the end but our relationship to the Lord.

Prayer: Lord, help me not to get too attached to this life. It will end far sooner than we think. In Jesus' Name, Amen.

NOVEMBER 13

Used of God

Isaiah 45:5 "I girded thee, though thou hast not known me."

God is speaking to Cyrus, the king of an ungodly nation, because He was going to use Cyrus to discipline His idol-worshiping people. God might use any person or circumstance to draw His people back to Him.

God wants to use us all who are His children. Though He did use Cyrus, a pagan, He only used Him once. He wants us to be used every day of our lives, and He will use us if we make ourselves available.

I was duck hunting late one afternoon with an old gun my daddy had received in a trade and gave to me. As I raised it to my shoulder and pushed the safety forward, it fired without my pulling the trigger. I wasn't ready for that!

Being used of God requires being ready. Read your Bible. Spend time in prayer. Keep your heart free of known sin. Be at peace with everyone. Use opportunities.

Prayer: Let me, Lord, be used in Your kingdom. For Jesus' sake, Amen.

NOVEMBER 14

God's Leadership

Isaiah 49:10 "Even by the springs of water shall He guide them."

The leading cow elk ahead of the herd, I am told, is one of the older ones that they trust. She leads them to water and food along a familiar trail and will be sensitive to danger.

Jesus said, "I am the good shepherd. My sheep know my voice and follow me." Right decisions in everyday life about vocation, business and even small things can be made if we let God lead. We don't have to plead for answers. God will show us where He is at work. All we have to do is join Him.

People who are sensitive to His leadership will notice a "check" in their spirit when they should wait or say "no." We can follow His leadership when we get to the point of having no will of our own. That gives us freedom to discern and follow His will alone.

Prayer: Lead, dear Lord. I will follow Your will in every circumstance, no matter what it costs. In Your Holy Name, Amen.

NOVEMBER 15

Chip Off the Old Block

Isaiah 51:1 "Look unto the rock whence ye are hewn."

We had two breeds of quail in our section of the country when I was growing up—bob whites and Mexican quail. I don't know how they got their names, but there was definitely a difference, though males in both groups said, "bob white." The so-called "Mexican" birds were smaller, but the coveys were bigger and they would often run further on the ground and flush ahead of the dogs more than the others did. That was genetics.

God, in our verse, was telling His people to look unto the rock they came from. In other words, they should get back to God. He had allowed them to become a large nation, and they had forsaken Him.

We were created by God to be a "chip off the old block," that is, to be like Him. The old folks would use that phrase when a child acted or looked like one of his parents. Can people look at you and say, "I know he is a child of God?"

Prayer: Lord, make me so that I look like You in the way I act and what I say. In Jesus' Name, Amen.

NOVEMBER 16

The Suffering Servant

Isaiah 53:3 "He is despised and rejected of men; a man of sorrows."

A badly deformed deer came walking through the woods one day. He was dragging one leg and looked like he had been in a fight, caught in a fence, or wounded by a hunter. We shot him to get him out of his suffering and were glad we did when we saw how badly he was infected. We were not able to keep the meat.

Jesus was the suffering servant who was God on earth. Isaiah 53 sounds like the whole chapter is from the New Testament because it describes what Jesus had to go through. Many people have suffered, so it is not unusual. What is so moving is that He sacrificed Himself for us.

Christians have to suffer, too. Jesus didn't take away the pain from Paul or the other disciples and He won't from us, but He says, "Lo, I am with you always, even to the end of the world." (Matthew 28:20)

Prayer: Lord, make me willing to suffer to follow You if I have to. In Jesus' Name, Amen.

NOVEMBER 17

Thirst

Isaiah 55:1 "Everyone that thirsteth, come ye to the waters . . ."

When we used to hunt quail, we would start about daylight, or as soon as we could get breakfast. We believed that the birds stirred early. We carried no water with us and usually had nothing to drink until we got back home at lunch. Since we were walking all of the time, we learned what the word "thirsty" meant.

People in the days of Isaiah would have understood, too, in that hot, dry part of the world. He kidded them about spending their money on things that didn't satisfy them and invited them to get free water that would quench their spiritual thirst.

They were restless, and I know something about that, too. For many years, I was not satisfied, no matter what I did. After I became willing to serve the Lord, I had peace. Things weren't perfect and still aren't, but my thirst is satisfied.

Prayer: Lord, I am thirsty, but I am accepting Your cool, satisfying water that lasts forever. Thank You. Amen.

NOVEMBER 18

God's Blessing

Isaiah 55:13 "Instead of the thorn shall come up the fir tree, and instead of the briar shall come up the myrtle tree."

Can you imagine rather than seeing does and spike bucks, you see trophies, or rather than finding one covey of quail, you find half a dozen? That really would be heaven, wouldn't it?

God promised Isaiah that He would reward faithful obedience by blessing them. Rather than worthless thorns and briars thriving, the valuable fir tree and beautiful myrtles would take their place.

He has the power to do just that. We can violate God's principles, but we deprive ourselves of God's blessings. Young people sometimes satisfy their lusts before marriage and, by doing so, damage their future marriage and remove God's hand of protection and blessing. Be patient and trust God. Your miracle of God's blessing will come.

Prayer: God, I am tempted to do it my way and bend the rules. I will wait on You. Amen.

NOVEMBER 19

A Place for All People

Isaiah 56:7 "For mine house shall be called an house of prayer for all people."

On our place there are many land tortoises. Now we call them "gophers," but I won't argue the point with Midwesterners today. They dig holes in the dirt and live down in there. I understand that snakes crawl in there and live with them. I guess since the gopher has such a hard shell, snakes can't bite them. Foxes and coyotes take the holes over sometimes, too. Several different animals may live there from one time to another.

Jesus overturned money changers' tables and drove them out with whips because the temple had become corrupt and commercialized. This was one of the very few times that Jesus got really angry. It was a place of prayer, and women and non-Jewish men were excluded.

Anyone who wants to worship should be allowed in God's house. Any race, nationality, gender, and saints and sinners alike should be allowed to worship. Only Christians who have professed Christ, commit to obey God's Word, and are baptized should become members.

Prayer: Lord, thank You for a sanctuary where we all can meet and freely worship. Amen.

NOVEMBER 20

When God Does Not Hear

Isaiah 59:2 "Your iniquities have separated between you and your God, and your sins have hid His face from you that he will not hear you."

I have hunted in a place near an interstate where you can't hear anything but cars and trucks. There are turkeys there, but you can't hear them gobble or yelp. You can't even hear deer walking on the dry leaves or squirrels barking.

The Bible says that there are things that keep God from hearing our prayers. Isaiah said that one of them separated Israel from God and caused Him to hide His face from them. It was their sin. They, apparently, were saying that God was unable to answer prayer and that He did not hear. Their sin was lack of faith.

When God does not answer your prayers, it could be because of known sin in your life. Be willing to forsake it, and He will cleanse you and begin answering your prayers, according to His will.

Prayer: Lord, forgive me, teach me to pray, and answer my prayers. In Jesus' Name, Amen.

NOVEMBER 21

Chosen

Isaiah 61:1 "The Spirit of the Lord is upon me; because the Lord hath anointed me to preach good tidings unto the meek."

When you hunt in some states, you have to apply for a license, and you may or may not get one. Several years ago, I applied to hunt in Montana and, to my surprise, they drew my name. I got all charged up and started making plans to go.

Our verse, and several after it, were quoted by Jesus in Luke 4:18 to announce His mission. God had sent His Son to minister to the spiritually needy and give good news of salvation. Being God, He had great power over disease, nature, and death, as well as the power to save us from our sins.

We as Christians are God's chosen people to do the same thing. The difference is that we cannot save. Are you a Christian? Then you have the spirit of the Lord on you and the power you need to serve Him.

Prayer: Lord, thank You that I am chosen and have the power to serve. In Jesus' Name, Amen.

NOVEMBER 22

One Reason Why Evil Comes

Isaiah 66:4 "I . . . will bring their fears upon them, because when I called, none did answer."

It is irritating to call your dog and not get any response. My bird dog used to hunt way out from me so that I couldn't see her at times. Sometimes she would point birds out there and I couldn't find her. She would hold her point like she was trained to do, but it made me mad anyway.

God calls us to do what He wants us to do, and we may ignore Him and do what we want to do. Our worst fears happen to us when we do that. It is not judgment; it is correction. We bring problems on ourselves when we turn a deaf ear to God.

Are you going through tough times? Are you in a hole and can't seem to get out? There are many reasons for that, but one could be found here. Listen closely. Have you intentionally been ignoring God? He may be trying to get your attention!

Prayer: Lord, bad things keep happening to me. I know that, if I need to change, You will not keep me in the dark. I am open. In Jesus' Name, Amen.

NOVEMBER 23

Important to God

Jeremiah 1:5 "Before I formed thee in the belly, I knew thee."

A hunter tells about killing a doe late in the season and how he felt to find an unborn fawn inside when he dressed her. He vowed never to shoot does again that late in the season. He seemed to feel as though he had violated holy territory. He had killed two deer at one shot.

Human babies are just as much human at conception as they will ever be. They aren't developed completely, but they are people just the same. Every human being is precious to God. Get this—He knew us before we were conceived. We are not accidents of human passion. Human parents, at times, act like they don't care about their children, and we see lots of abuse and neglect.

My wife, Martha, teaches in elementary school and sees cases of unwanted and unloved children who grew up rebellious, thinking nobody loves them. You may be one of those. Good news—God created you out of love to fill an important place that only you can fill. You are important. As a Christian, you can be a "child of the king."

Prayer: Lord, thank you that I have something to give me hope. You love me. Thank You, again. Amen.

NOVEMBER 24

Inadequate

Jeremiah 1:6 "Then said I, "Ah, Lord God, behold I cannot speak for I am but a child."

Little fawns are so helpless. They can run by the time they hit the ground, but they are small, weak and a little unstable. They would be defenseless against a panther, coyote, or even a bobcat, so they are hidden by their mothers in thick places and they lie motionless for hours.

God called Jeremiah as a teenager to be a "prophet to the nations." He didn't feel worthy or capable to take on such a big job. In Jeremiah chapter one, verse eight, God tells him, "Be not afraid, I am with thee to deliver thee." Moses had those same kinds of feelings and God told him the same thing. They both did all God wanted them to do, and He never let them down.

You may know God wants you to do something, but you feel the way Jeremiah and Moses did. You are right, and He doesn't want you to depend on what you can do. Just surrender and God will do it through you. I feel so inadequate to preach, and every time I enter a pulpit I have to say, "Lord, You will have to do this through me."

Prayer: Lord, this is too big for me, but not for You. I will let You do it through me. I surrender. Amen.

NOVEMBER 25

Correction

Jeremiah 2:19 "Thine own wickedness shall correct thee and thy backsliding shall reprove thee."

Bucks that are usually cautious sometimes become careless during the rut. At other times, they feed at night and find a thick place to bed down during the day. They usually travel alone in our part of the country. When the hormones begin to flow, they will follow a doe or several does and the number attracts the hunter's attention. Bucks will sometimes even travel in broad daylight, to their doom.

God warned that backsliding (turning from godliness to un-godliness), brings on its own judgment. A person who reads "girly" magazines is in trouble and inviting bigger trouble. One drink of alcohol can lead to a wreck and death. Foolish spending can lead to poverty, which could lead to drug abuse, which may even lead to robbery and murder. Harsh words can start an agonizing journey toward divorce.

Giving in to temptation will slap you in the face and come back to haunt you. Don't take that first step. The laws of nature are unforgiving, and human weakness that is not harnessed will destroy any of us.

Prayer: Lord, give me strength beyond my strength to say, "no," when I must. In Jesus' Name, Amen.

NOVEMBER 26

The Slippery Slope

Jeremiah 3:22 "Return, ye backsliding children, and I will heal your backsliding."

One day I was watching a squirrel feeding and playing around in the trees. They can usually go to the end of a limb and jump to a limb on another tree. That day, one miscalculated and didn't quite reach the next limb. He hit on a weak bough, slipped, and fell all the way to the ground. He landed on his feet and wasn't hurt. Some people backslide in their faith and aren't so lucky. It causes great damage.

The word "backsliding" was in yesterday's lesson. On another occasion, Jeremiah said that Israel was like a wife who had left her husband. At one time they were faithful but had let other things cloud their minds that distracted them. He promised to get them on the right path if they would return to Him.

You may remember when you were an altar boy, attended Bible school, or went to church with your parents and now you hardly ever go to church or think of God. You are backslidden, or maybe you are spiritually dead and in real danger. You may feel guilty at times. You need to meet God halfway. Don't continue down that "slippery slope." You can do yourself and your loved ones great harm from the fall.

Prayer: I can't call You "Lord" because I don't live for You. I want to serve You and will start going to church. For Jesus' sake, Amen.

NOVEMBER 27

A High Risk Life

Jeremiah 5:12 "It is not He (the Lord), neither shall evil come upon us."

All hunters know that at the beginning of dove season, the doves fly lower and slower. Sometimes they light on power lines or fields close by. They have become so accustomed to people, tractors, and other animals in the fields that they let their guard down and take more risk. Young birds hatched the same year just don't know any better.

Israel had gotten the same way. God had been so good to them that they didn't expect Him to punish evil. Their disobedience finally caught up with them, and their enemies destroyed their land and took many away to a foreign land.

Many people today see God as a kind of permissive "gray-headed grandfather" who tolerates and overlooks our high risk lives. He is very patient, but His holy nature cannot let sin continue. As He judged Israel, He will judge us as a nation and as individuals. We will have to give account for every idle word.

Prayer: Lord, help me to examine my life and clean it up before You have to judge me. In Jesus' Name, Amen.

NOVEMBER 28

Do Not Pray for Them

Jeremiah 7:16 "Pray not thou for this people . . . for I will not hear."

I heard the story of a quail hunter hunting in South Georgia with his prized dog. The dog pointed some distance away, suddenly yelped in pain, and cowered away from his point. The hunter suddenly realized what had happened. The poor animal had been bitten by a rattlesnake. Being so far from a veterinarian, there was no hope, and the dog soon died.

God told Jeremiah not to pray for Israel anymore because He would not answer and save them. They had gone too far and waited too long. There is a time when God will no longer hear prayer. Genesis 6:3 says, "God will not strive with man forever."

It is a frightening thought that at some point, God would not hear our prayers for others or others' prayers for us. I guess God knows that it would do no good. Sometimes, hard-headed people have to learn the hard way. Turn around while you have some desire to do it. Hell is a high price to pay for delaying too long.

Prayer: Lord, draw me back closer to You. I can hardly hear You speak, and I don't want to go too far. In Jesus' Name, Amen.

NOVEMBER 29

What to Value

Jeremiah 9:23 "Let not the wise man glory in his wisdom, neither let the mighty man glory in his might, let not the rich man glory in his riches . . ."

We are living in a very materialistic world, and it is easy to get caught up in it. Many people spend tons of money and a great deal of time in sporting goods stores, getting the latest goose calls, camouflage equipment and such. If that becomes an obsession that monopolizes our time and drains us of money that our family needs for necessities, our priorities are wrong.

There are many good things, like hunting, wisdom, strength, and wealth, but anything we put ahead of God is sin.

You can tell pretty easily what you are glorying in. Is your spouse complaining about the time you spend away from home? Do you run short of funds to pay bills so much that your wife has to put the kids in day school and go to work because you spent too much on hunting? How much time do you give to the Lord? We value what we spend our time, effort, and money on.

Prayer: Lord, I just realized that my priorities are wrong. Help me get back on track. In Jesus' Name, Amen.

NOVEMBER 30

A Deceitful Heart

Jeremiah 17:9 "The heart is deceitful above all things, and desperately wicked."

My son and a friend were deer hunting on our place one day, and the friend vowed that he saw a mountain lion walk by his stand. Nothing we said could convince him otherwise. I called some people who should know, and they confirmed that a few lions had been released in the state to see how they would get along with livestock. They could have asked anybody and saved themselves lots of trouble. A mountain lion will invite a calf, pig, goat, or maybe even the farmer's daughter over for lunch! They can't be trusted. They are big, aggressive, and often hungry.

God says that humans can't be trusted either–none of us are above doing just about anything if given the chance.

The lesson is "never say never." Neither you nor I are exempt. Don't trust yourself to be around tempting things and resist. Avoid tempting things, and when you are being pulled in the wrong direction, go the other way. You might be able to resist most things, but you have a weakness, and Satan will exploit it.

Prayer: Lord, I am weak. Give me the courage to realize I am being tempted and to run. In Jesus' Name, Amen.

DECEMBER 1

Clay in God's Hands

Jeremiah 18:6 "As clay is in the potter's hand, so are ye in mine hand."

Taxidermists can do some amazing things with hides and heads. They can take antlers from one deer and skin from another and make it look like it was all one deer. I don't understand how they can mount an entire bird or animal so that you can't tell where the skin was cut.

Jeremiah was given a lesson by God as he watched a potter making something out of clay. The clay was hard to shape, so the potter took it off the wheel, tore it up and made something beautiful out of it. God can make a useful vessel out of a person, too.

Have you made a mess of things and wonder if you can ever be right with God or be used of God in any way? The answer is "yes," on one condition. Will you yield your life to Him?

Prayer: Let me be clay in Your hands, and please shape me like You want to. Thank You. Amen.

DECEMBER 2

Prayer and the Law

Jeremiah 21:2 "Inquire, I pray thee, of the Lord for us."

If Christians decide to violate hunting laws, they need not pray that God will protect them from the law. A person who does things like that is on his own.

Babylon was about to attack Israel, so King Zedekiah sent for Jeremiah that he might pray for them. He did, but God replied that he would fight for Babylon against Israel, defeat them, and even King Zedekiah would not be spared. Israel had disobeyed God continuously, and He was bringing disaster on them.

The same kinds of things happen to Christians as non-Christians if they do the same ungodly things. Natural and civil laws apply to everyone. The old saying is, "We sow our wild oats and hope for a crop failure."

Prayer: Lord, let my prayers come from an innocent heart so You will answer them. In Jesus' Name, Amen.

DECEMBER 3

A Warning for the Man of God

Jeremiah 23:1 "Woe be unto the pastors that destroy and scatter the sheep of my pasture."

Many people are concerned about the environment, and particularly the preservation of wildlife. They believe that outlawing hunting would solve the problem. Insurance companies might disagree. There are a rising number of claims because of wrecks with deer. Most hunters are conservationists and foot the bill for protecting wildlife, but let us remember that we must keep up the good work or we will not have game to hunt.

God gives a warning to pastors or protectors of His flock. A pastor called to be a shepherd of a church should be like the "Good Shepherd," Jesus. He would lay down his life for the church. Many, however, have strayed from the truth. Others can't get along with people or are lazy.

I encourage people to support good pastors, but substandard ones should be confronted privately and in a non-threatening way. If you are a pastor, be worthy of the calling. If you are one who is critical of every pastor you ever had, you need to apologize and repent.

Prayer: Lord, thank You for good pastors. Protect them from critics, and guide them to serve well. For Your kingdom's sake, Amen.

DECEMBER 4

False Prophets

Jeremiah 23:32 "Behold, I am against them that prophesy false dreams, saith the Lord."

A good hunting guide can be worth his weight in gold, and you usually have to pay a lot of gold to get one. The only time I used one for elk, he put us where we saw some. Our chances would have been small without the guide, since we did not know the area or the habits of elk. We need guidance for life as well, but we need to be careful that we get the right kind.

A false prophet in Israel didn't last long. If his prophecies didn't come true, he lost his life. God used many true prophets in the Old Testament to tell His truth.

Preaching is very serious business. People who preach and teach the Bible should be careful that they teach the truth. Leading people astray has eternal consequences. If you are a teacher, you need to study hard with commentaries and pray for God to speak through you.

Prayer: Lord, help me to learn how to tell truth from error when I hear the Bible taught, and may I teach Your Word accurately. In Jesus' Name, Amen.

DECEMBER 5

Not Hard to Find

Jeremiah 29:13 "Ye shall seek me and find me when ye search for me with all your heart."

We can hunt half a day now and find no coveys of quail where we used to find several. Some say it is because of bad habitat, pesticides, predators, or other things, but I am not sure we really know. One thing I do know, coveys of wild birds are extremely hard to find.

God isn't. He does not force Himself on anyone, and if we want to go along without Him, He will let us. He will even discipline His people and judge the lost to try to bring them to Him because He wants an intimate relationship with everyone.

The ball is in our court. If we aren't close to Him, it isn't God's fault. Are you getting closer to Him? If you want to be, pray more, read His Word more, serve Him, and be faithful in worship. That is a good start.

Prayer: You are easy to find, Lord. You aren't playing hide-and-seek. Help me to want a closer relationship with You. In Jesus' Name, Amen.

DECEMBER 6

Unfaithful

Ezekiel 16:26 "Thou hast also committed fornication."

Hunters used to have a name for a female dog that I won't even write down. It is crude and carries the idea that she did not care what male dog was near when she came "in season," and she did not discriminate. The same word has been used as a slur against unfaithful and boisterous women.

Ezekiel used another blunt word, "fornication," to describe Israel's behavior and their dependence on Assyria rather than God. God warned them of doom because of it.

Anyone would be angry enough to bite nails in two if they were to be described that way, but unfaithfulness to Him is called that out of God's own mouth. He has strong feelings about unfaithfulness.

Prayer: God, help me to be true to You, my spouse, and all my commitments. May I never deserve to be referred to as a "fornicator." In Jesus' Name, Amen.

DECEMBER 7

Death

Ezekiel 18:4 "The soul that sinneth, it shall die."

We hear about so many tragedies of children and adults being shot or even killed by a gun that was not supposed to be loaded. There is a rule among hunters never to take a loaded gun into the house. Many violate that rule, but it is a high price to pay when there is an injury or death because of carelessness or insensitivity.

God warns us through Ezekiel that sin causes death, yet we continue to willfully break the law of God. We do it and don't see an immediate bolt of lightning and feel like we got away with something.

Physical death may not come when we sin, though it could, but we die a little bit spiritually every time. Every sin places scars on our souls, hardens our hearts, and separates us from God. Some of us get so far that we have no conscience and don't hear God's voice anymore. That is spiritual death.

Prayer: Lord, help me turn back before I go too far. In Jesus' Name, Amen.

DECEMBER 8

Bearing Iniquity

Ezekiel 18:20 "The son shall not bear the iniquity of the father, nor the father for the son."

Armadillos have become a nuisance. You can see them from your deer stand digging up the ground looking for worms, and that is fine. When it becomes a problem is when they get in your wife's flower bed and destroy it. You can catch the rascals, I am told, by sticking a piece of eight inch PVC pipe at an angle in the ground and putting a cup of fish bait worms in the bottom. The guilty party gets in and can't back out.

Sometimes we have to suffer for what a parent or a child does. When they get in trouble, we hurt, too. An ungodly child can cause gray hair in a hurry. Things our forefathers did, like slavery, still haunt us. Bad influences are hard to overcome, but you can.

The good and bad news is that we aren't responsible for what others do, unless we lead them astray, but we are responsible for what we do. Under God, this old saying is true, "Every tub has to sit on its own bottom."

Prayer: Lord, thank You that I don't have to pay the price for the sins of others, but please deliver me from my sin and bad influences in my life. Thank You that You do. Amen.

DECEMBER 9

Standing Strong

Ezekiel 22:30 "I sought for a man among them that could . . . stand in the gap for me."

We read stories regularly about some hunter who got between a bear and her cubs by mistake. If the old sow feels that you are about to mess with her little ones, you are in real trouble. You'd better get out of there in a hurry.

God was seeking someone who would "stand in the gap," that is, stand up for what was right, like the bear will for her cubs. God saw oppression, robbery, and mistreatment of the poor and strangers, and found no one in Israel to help them, so he punished Israel.

God is looking for people today who will stand strong for the innocent, underdogs, and the mistreated. Further, He wants people who will believe and obey Him, be honest and truthful, and resist temptation. Many Christians are collapsing under the pressure of what everyone else is doing, rather than standing strong.

Prayer: Lord, I want to stand strong for the sake of my family, church, nation, and You. Help me. Amen.

DECEMBER 10

Warnings

Ezekiel 33:5 "He that taketh warning shall deliver his soul."

Most animals have a warning system to survive. Geese will honk loudly, deer will snort or blow, squirrels will bark, and for others, the signal is the flapping of wings or the pounding of hoofs as they escape danger. One who fails to respond to warnings may suffer the consequences.

This story holds the watchman accountable if he doesn't warn the people. It is similar to how sentries in the army are held responsible. Those warned are themselves responsible if they don't heed the warnings.

There are warnings in the Bible, through words of other people, and through the mistakes made by others. Wise people in business and life in general succeed by following good judgment. We see people dying around us every day, yet some people fail to heed the warning of dying without Jesus. We can save our souls by heeding spiritual warnings.

Prayer: Lord, I will listen to Your warnings and heed them. Thank You. Amen.

DECEMBER 11

Purity

Daniel 1:8 "Daniel purposed in his heart that he would not defile himself."

My first bird dog, Belle, was a very good one right from the start, but she had one little problem. She absolutely would not get in water. It was a little inconvenient to have to pick her up and carry her across every time we came to a little stream, since she weighed about fifty pounds. I guess she didn't want to get her feet wet. One day, I just threw her in and she was fine after that.

Daniel's Jewish diet didn't include meats that the Babylonians ate. It was probably because it had been a burnt offering for their gods. Though it might cost him his life, he refused to eat it. He didn't want to be tainted by something that was unclean to him, just like Belle did not want to get her feet wet.

I wish we had that kind of conviction these days. Illegal drugs, alcohol, tobacco, and such are even used by Christians. They also do things that are ungodly. God would bless us and we would feel better about ourselves if we would decide to be pure.

Prayer: Lord, I do things that I need to stop. With Your help, I will. In Christ's Name, Amen.

DECEMBER 12

Trusting God

Daniel 3:17 "Our God whom we serve is able to deliver us from the burning fiery furnace."

Three young Jewish boys would not worship the king's idols, and he threatened throwing them in a furnace. They would not obey his command and told him God would rescue them. He threw them in the fire and they didn't burn, but the guards who put them in the fire were burned up.

It had flooded, and the branches were full of water. I was in a hurry to get home from a hunt and was debating whether to drive across a flooded muddy branch, which would save me a couple of miles. If I bogged down, it would make me late for sure. I did risk it, and, thank the Lord, my four wheel drive and mud grips brought me through. Faith in my truck paid off.

There are times when we have a choice of trusting God and being obedient about tithing, going on a mission trip to a dangerous country, witnessing to someone we don't know, or something else. God has always been faithful when I have stretched myself to serve Him.

Prayer: Lord, give me the power to obey when You challenge me to trust You. In Jesus' Name, Amen.

DECEMBER 13

Dealing With Unfaithfulness

Hosea 3:1 "Go love a woman beloved of her friend, yet an adulteress."

A hunter I once knew would leave very early in the morning to go hunting. As soon as he was out of sight, a neighbor would go to his house and "visit" his wife. He apparently never knew about it, but the rest of the community did. If he knew, he forgave her and went on.

Hosea's wife bore him three children, one of which probably wasn't his. She then left to become a prostitute. As a model of His love for His people, God commanded Hosea to go claim her when she had become old, been rejected by her lovers, and put on the auction block.

That would be a hard thing to take—an unfaithful spouse. It would require love that is bigger than I am. God loves us that much. We have sinned, even willfully, and when we return to Him, He forgives. If we have that kind of love, we can forgive a spouse or anyone else.

Prayer: Lord, I hope I never have to experience an unfaithful wife. Give me grace to forgive if I do. In Jesus' Name, Amen.

DECEMBER 14

God's Spirit to Come

Joel 2:28 "I will pour my spirit upon all flesh."

There is nothing more exciting than sitting in a dove field when, all of a sudden, the sky is black with doves. You are shooting as fast as you can until you don't have time to pick up dead birds. That is rare these days, but old folks used to tell about having two guns and someone picking up birds and reloading guns for them.

The Old Testament tells us how man tried to please God by burning animals and even children. Occasionally, the Spirit of God would come upon a person and he would have a sudden burst of energy, would be filled with excitement, and be able to do great things for God.

Joel spoke for God and told us that the Spirit would come. Hundreds of years later, He did, and nothing is more exciting than knowing He will come into our lives, forgive us, and direct our lives if we will let Him.

Prayer: Thank you, Lord, for the thrill it is when You come into our lives and live through us. Amen.

DECEMBER 15

Seeking God

Amos 5:4 "Seek ye me and ye shall live."

God contrasts seeking Him with a person running from a lion and meeting a bear or getting home and getting a snakebite in his house. That is quite a situation. When we run from the Lord, we find ourselves not being able to deal with the problems of life.

His Word keeps saying, "Seek me and live," or "Seek good and not evil and live." Everybody wants a good life, full of happiness and peace. God says the way we get that is through Him. One of my brothers talks about the Bible being the "manufacturer's handbook." If you want your car to run right and last long, you use the handbook. Follow God's handbook and life goes smoother.

How are you going about making yourself and your family happy? First, you can't make *anybody* happy. Keep on running from the Lord, and you will fail. Seek God and encourage your family to do the same, and if they do, they will find true happiness.

Prayer: Help me, Lord, to seek You and really live. In Jesus' Name, Amen.

DECEMBER 16

The Call of God

Jonah 3:1 "The word of the Lord came to Jonah a second time."

Getting up early even to deer hunt is very hard. You know you need to be up the stand before daylight, but you know it is cold, and that bed feels mighty good. After you get moving, it's a piece of cake. The same is true with obeying God's call.

Jonah the prophet had been called by God to preach to some very wicked people. They were Jonah's enemies, and he didn't want God to save them, so he went in the opposite direction and was thrown overboard a ship and swallowed by a large fish. He came to his senses and obeyed God the second time. Many people were saved.

God called me to ministry at age fourteen, but because I wanted power, position, and money, I just put it off until I was in my mid-thirties. That made it harder on me and my family. It is easier to be obedient at the time God first calls. Is He calling you to do something? Don't put it off.

Prayer: Lord, help me to be honest with myself and just go on and do what I know You want me to do. In Jesus' Name, Amen.

DECEMBER 17

God's Ways

Micah 4:2 "Let us go up to the mountain of the Lord . . . and He will teach us His ways."

I guess I learned more about accurate shooting in the army than anywhere else. It has come in handy when hunting. They teach you methods of holding the rifle steady by shooting from different positions, proper breathing patterns, bracing your thumb against your cheek, sight alignment, etc. Their way is not the only way, but I think it is best. The drill sergeant thinks so, too.

Micah encouraged the people to go to the mountain of God to learn His ways. Why? Wouldn't the One who created us know how we should live? He saw the pagan world in his day and the destructiveness and futility of it. God's ways are best. Look around you and see what the alternatives are, and you will agree.

The first thing we need is a true desire to know God, then everything else falls in place. We will go to the house of the Lord, read our Bible, and pray. God will honor that and lead us closer to Him every day.

Prayer: Lord, give me the desire to know You. In Jesus' Name, Amen.

DECEMBER 18

God's Glory

Habakkuk 2:14 "For the earth shall be filled with the knowledge of the glory of the Lord."

Have you ever been confronted by a skunk? They look harmless enough, and I don't know whether they bite or not, but they can let their presence be known. Our dogs used to try to catch one every now and then when we were hunting coons and possums at night. The dogs lived to regret it. The odor a skunk sends out is foul and hard to remove.

Our verse today prophesied that God's glory would be made known all over the world. It is like sweet perfume. It is a clear warning to evil people who oppress and harm others but good news to those who obey the Lord.

The Book of Romans in the New Testament tells us that God reveals Himself through His creation. However, people fail to worship Him and, instead, worship what He created. Then, they lapse into immoral living, lying, gossiping, envy, ill will, etc. How have you responded to glory that God has revealed to you?

Prayer: Lord, help me to see Your glory and worship You. In Jesus' Name, Amen.

DECEMBER 19

Rejoicing in the Lord

Habakkuk 3:18 "Yet I will rejoice in the Lord, I will joy in the God of my salvation."

Wood ducks are exciting to hunt, because you can hear their shrill yelp long before they arrive. Drama builds as you hear their call, then the whistle of their wings, and then you see them coming with blinding speed. It is really fun when you make a good shot and one falls.

The old prophet said that he trembled because of his troubles. Though armies were invading and the fruit trees weren't blossoming and bearing fruit, he would still rejoice in the Lord. He had his faith in the right place. When we do, it will give us real and lasting joy.

An older, godly man asked a friend, "How are you doing?" "I'm doing fine under the circumstances," was the ready reply. The older man answered back, "What are you doing down there under those circumstances?" The point was well made. Sometimes the circumstances of life get us down, when we should be focused on the Lord, trusting Him and rejoicing.

Prayer: Lord, help me trust You more and rejoice, even when things are tough. You have already won the victory. In Jesus' Name, Amen.

DECEMBER 20

Our Ways

Haggai 1:7 "Consider Your Ways."

Bobcats have a way about them that works well in catching their prey. They usually walk very quietly, and you can hardly hear them on dry leaves. They detect movement and stand motionless to determine if noise is coming from a threat to them or a candidate for food. Then they crouch low, focus on the prey, and slide on their belly until the unsuspecting victim is in range.

Haggai was challenging the people to build the house of the Lord. They lived in luxury, and God's house was in ruins. They were neglecting Him. Nothing they did was succeeding because God wasn't blessing them. They had everything but were not satisfied. Haggai was saying, "Wake up!"

We have lots of things and are involved in many "fun" activities but aren't content and at peace. We are restless, unhappy and irritable. What is wrong? Consider what you are focused on. Is it God? When we get our priorities in agreement with His will, He blesses us, and we are at peace.

Prayer: Lord, help me take a new look at myself. I want to live for You. In Jesus' Name, Amen.

DECEMBER 21

Who Owns You?

Haggai 2:8 "The silver is mine and the gold is mine saith the Lord."

When I had just bought a certain small piece of property, I went before the hunting season to scout it out. There were several nice deer stands on it that belonged to someone else. Since I didn't know who owned them, I wrote a note and said, "Today these are your stands. Tomorrow they are mine." They disappeared soon.

God says something we already know, if we think about it. Everything belongs to Him. He created it and He owns it all, even us. Paul says in 1 Corinthians 6:20, " . . . ye are bought with a price."

That is what Christianity is about. He came to save us. We were always His by creation, but now we can be His by rebirth. Are you really His?

Prayer: Lord, I realize now that I own nothing, including myself. I'm glad to belong to You. Thank You. Amen.

DECEMBER 22

Turn to Me

Zechariah 1:3 "Turn ye unto me, saith the Lord of hosts and I will turn unto you."

The right kind of hunting is good stewardship. When we provide quality food and habitat, it comes back to us in successful hunting. If we neglect those things, game will move to a better location or cease to exist.

It is like turning to God. If we do, God will focus on us and bless us. If we want to live without Him, He will let us. God is waiting for us to make the first move. Actually, He made the first move by coming to die on the cross.

An "Untitled" song written by Chris Rice says, "Weak and wounded sinner, left alone to die, O lift your head, the Son is passing by. Come to Jesus and live." Haven't you turned your back on Him long enough?

Prayer: Lord, I'm tired of living without You. I invite You into my heart now. In Jesus' Name, Amen.

DECEMBER 23

A Holy Time

Zechariah 2:13 "Be silent, O all flesh, before the Lord."

Most hunting requires dead silence. Oh, people talk and even whistle and call out to each other in a dove field and even quail hunting. Noisy people are not likely to see deer, elk, or some other animals.

Zechariah tells us to be silent before the Lord for several reasons: so He can speak to us, to remember our unworthiness, or sometimes, to observe Him at work. He is holy and righteous and we are so much the opposite.

Christmas is too often boisterous, materialistic, and irreverent. It is okay for children to get excited about presents and for adults to enjoy the fellowship of family and friends, but we should take time to be silent before the Lord. Be still!

Prayer: Lord, You are so holy and Christmas is so holy. We worship You! Amen.

DECEMBER 24

The Power to Succeed

Zechariah 4:6 "Not by might . . . but my Spirit saith the Lord."

"Buck fever" is common among young deer hunters and some older ones. To a young hunter, even a spike buck looks huge. My son, when he was very young, was on the truck with a shotgun loaded with buck shot when three eight point bucks ran by him. He didn't fire a shot. He had all the firepower he needed, but the "spirit" to shoot wasn't there. He had a bad case of buck fever.

God tells us in our verse for today that man's muscle, resources, and intelligence cannot win the important battles of life. It will be His Spirit. He is moving in the lives of people to save them, and when we are obediently following His leadership, we will succeed. Christmas reminds us that He came and brought victory.

The power to succeed in life doesn't always come to those who are the strongest, the most intelligent, or the wealthiest. The powerful hand of God moves and tips the scales. Put your faith in Him and do your best. He will accomplish what He wants to through you!

Prayer: Lord, I am glad that Your power, not my ability, will bring me success. Thank You. Amen.

DECEMBER 25

Gifts to God

Malachi 1:8 "And if ye offer the blind for sacrifice, is it not evil?"

Would you even think of going into the woods to hunt without good camouflage, guns and equipment? Many hunters feel that they have to have the best available. A man's pride is at stake, you know! If we go on one of our big game hunts, we have to have special calls, scents, clothing, and maybe a new gun.

Malachi saw his people offering blind and lame animals as sacrifices to Holy God and called it "evil." Priests of God dishonored His name. Judaism, in those days, had stooped to new lows. No wonder God did not speak through His prophets for over four hundred years after Malachi.

What are you giving to God this Christmas? We splurge for our family and a good thing has gotten out of hand. Churches are often taking missions offerings before Christmas. What did you give to that? Did you give your best, or the leftovers?

Prayer: Lord, I owe You the first and best. Deliver me from giving You the leftovers. In Jesus' Name, Amen.

DECEMBER 26

The Trailblazer

Malachi 3:1 "Behold, I will send my messenger, and he shall prepare the way."

The place we hunt deer a lot is very thick with bushes and vines in some places. Since deer use the path of least resistance, we cut wide trails to channel them in our direction. This prepares a way for them to go from their bedding areas to our food plots.

God would send His Son, Jesus, but John the Baptist was sent first to make preparations. Malachi prophesied about it hundreds of years beforehand. John went into the background when Jesus came, but he introduced Jesus as the "Lamb of God which taketh away the sin of the world." (John 1:29)

We are trailblazers. People will follow us—our children, friends and family, and people we don't even know. The message of a song named "May All Who Come Behind Us Find Us Faithful," sung by Steve Green, asks us an important question. What kind of trail are you leaving?

Prayer: Lord, continuing with the song, "may the footprints that we leave, lead them to believe." That is my prayer, for Jesus' sake, Amen.

DECEMBER 27

The One to Come

Malachi 3:3 "And He shall sit as a refiner and purifier of silver."

Many years ago, I understand, deer that are much larger than the ones in our area were released here to "refine" and improve our herd. I can't verify that, but I did kill a large buck in the release area that was bigger field dressed than any of our native deer.

The verse for today continues to talk of One to come who would refine and purify. In other places in the Bible, He would be called "Savior, Lord of Lords, King of Kings, Everlasting Father, and Prince of Peace." He came at Christmas two thousand years ago, and His name was Jesus.

The One "who has come" does not benefit some people, because they have not allowed Him to come to them. Has He come to you? He will, if you ask Him, and you will be pure. Why not now?

Prayer: Lord, come to live in me, and control my life. In Jesus' Name, Amen.

DECEMBER 28

The Unchangeable God

Malachi 3:6 "I am the Lord, I change not."

Quail are relatively easy to hit. When you get over the noise of their wings, get used to their speed, and learn how to lead them, it is a piece of cake. That is saying a lot, but seriously, they fly in a straight line at a constant speed, unlike doves.

God "flies" straight, too, and doesn't change because He has no need to. He has always been complete and perfect. His Word, the Bible, is not outdated by time and is still valid. He doesn't have to adjust because He has always seen past, present, and future all at the same time. He is never taken by surprise.

We are different and need to change. We will never get to the point when we won't. Christians continue to see new ways to obey God and alter their lives to be more like Jesus. Some people resist change because they fear the unknown. Don't be afraid to change. There is a whole new world out there.

Prayer: Lord, show me how I need to change and give me the power to do it. I am willing and will try hard. In Jesus' Name, Amen.

DECEMBER 29

Robbing God

Malachi 3:8 "Will a man rob God?"

Some birds will rob the eggs from nests of other birds and eat them. Chicken snakes will, too. In the spring, you can see birds chasing crows, which are the worst kind of robbers, across the sky to get them away from their nests.

I understand why those things happen, but how can a man rob God? How could a person have the gall to do it? Maybe it is ignorance. When we keep something that belongs to God, we rob Him, whether it is of our time, talent, opportunity, or money.

If we spend these on ourselves, we rob Him. We are not created for ourselves but to serve God and others. Are you robbing Him? What are you doing with what you have?

Prayer: O God, I have been keeping things for myself that I know now are Yours. I am sorry and will obey You. Thank You for all You have given me. Amen.

DECEMBER 30

The Lord's Tithe

Malachi 3:10 "Bring ye all the tithes into the storehouse."

A hunting club I heard about had a member that would not pay his dues. He would kill deer that violated the rules because he declared them "damaging and substandard for the herd." He would not pay the fines the club had set for violations. Finally, he was dismissed from the club.

It is a commandment of God that we give at least a tenth of all we earn to the church. He promises, as it were, to open the "windows of heaven" and bless us if we do. In Malachi 3:9, He said that if we don't we are "cursed with a curse."

Many Christians do not obey God and tithe. Even if they give a tenth, some designate part of it for causes of their choice. That is not tithing. The tithe is for the church, according to the Bible. It is not ours to designate. Nothing we possess is ours, not even the ninety percent we have left. He gave us health and opportunity to earn all of it.

Prayer: Lord, I own nothing. It is Yours. I willingly obey with gratitude. Thank You. Amen.

DECEMBER 31

Healing Broken Relationships

Malachi 4:6 "He shall turn the heart of the fathers to their children and the heart of the children to their fathers."

Some types of birds and other wildlife travel around in groups. Quail go in coveys and elk in herds. I doubt that it has anything to do with tender feelings or loving family relationships. Survival is probably the reason.

God ordained the family to live together harmoniously. The Bible teaches that God can restore broken family relationships. It is His will for families to love one another and get along well together. If there are broken relationships, it is because the parties involved are not right with God.

I know of many broken marriages, children who are at odds with parents, and children who are not speaking to each other. They won't make things right because they can't. The first step is getting right with God. If people draw near to God, they will get closer to one another.

New Year's Eve would be a great time to make some phone calls or step across the room and say, "I am sorry." God can put things back together.

Prayer: Lord, break down barriers between You and me, so they can come down between me and my family. For Jesus' sake, Amen.

TATE PUBLISHING, LLC

Tate Publishing is committed to excellence in the publishing industry. Our staff of highly trained professionals—editors, graphic designers, and marketing personnel—work together to produce the very finest book products available. The company reflects in every aspect the philosophy established by the founders based on Psalms 68:11, "The Lord gave the word and great was the company of those who published it."

If you would like further information, please call
1.888.361.9473
or visit our website at
www.tatepublishing.com

Tate Publishing LLC
127 E. Trade Center Terrace
Mustang, Oklahoma 73064 USA